introduction to
Rock &
Moun-
tain
Climb-
ing

by Ruth & John Mendenhall

introduction to Rock & Mountain Climbing

Illustrated by Vivian Mendenhall

STACKPOLE BOOKS

INTRODUCTION TO ROCK AND
MOUNTAIN CLIMBING

Published by
STACKPOLE BOOKS
Cameron and Kelker Streets
Harrisburg, Pa. 17105

Standard Book Number 8117-0922-1
Library of Congress Catalog Card Number 69-16148
Printed in U.S.A.

Contents

chapter one

The Sport of Mountain Climbing

TO most people mountains are two-dimensional scenery, as pretty as color pictures and no more real. To a small number of men and women, however, each peak is a solid, unique, three-dimensional entity. These few find in the mountains fundamentals that give deep meaning and joy to their lives beyond and above all ordinary pursuits. They are the ones who climb.

And what is mountain climbing, besides getting to the top of peaks under your own power? The sport has many facets. Non-technical ascents resemble uphill hikes, often long and strenuous. They require little more than energy and good outdoor common sense—including the judgment to know where the non-technical climbing stops and the technical begins. Technical climbing means climbing with a rope and other equipment on terrain that is hazardous without protection. Between the two types there is some overlap. Hiking and backpacking are involved in the approach to most technical climbs. Some peaks have both easy and difficult routes to the summit, or the route itself is a mixture of climbing problems. Non-technical climbing often provides background skills, knowledge, and inspiration for learning about technical aspects of the sport.

Technical climbing is of two kinds. Rock climbing refers to scaling cliffs with the protection of equipment and special techniques. It is frequently an exuberant end in itself, but may also be an integral part of major ascents. In snow, ice, and glacier work, ropes are also used for protection. Some of the techniques are similar to those used on rock, but most of the equipment is different. Both rock climbing, and snow and ice climbing, have their partisans and specialists. Many climbers, especially those of long experience, have an intense interest and competence in all phases of mountain climbing. These are the mountaineers.

Roped climbing is a poorly understood sport in the United States, where people say things to climbers like: "You must be Swiss (or French)—you are wearing one of those hats (or baggy pants)."

Or, "*I* could never do that; heights make me want to jump off."

Or, "But you don't *look* like a mountain climber."

Or, most frequently, "You ought to give up climbing. It is too dangerous!"

Climbers do not think of themselves as curiosities or suicidal crackpots, nor of their sport as a sensation. With such a general reaction to climbing, it is no wonder that its enthusiasts become rather reticent and withdrawn with outsiders (except perhaps for promoting the sensation theory through photography).

A swimmer, skier, or ball player does not become really good at his sport without a bent for it, and long training in muscle skills and techniques. A climber too finds that a natural flair is helpful—but is indispensable only for outstanding proficiency. Almost anyone can learn to climb competently if he is fired with sufficient zeal and desire to put forth the effort. He must develop skills in specialized, complicated, and sometimes controversial techniques, through both instruction and long practice. He must become familiar with equipment, its evolution, and how to use it. He must gain a detailed knowledge of constantly changing natural conditions. If he seeks really challenging ascents, he must prepare for extreme physical demands. He must possess a high degree of determination and willpower. And he must be able to judge his own capacities and those of the people he climbs with.

When all this knowledge, drive, and experience are fused together, the climber is far safer on potentially dangerous cliffs or glaciers than a careless hiker is on a trail. It should be reassuring to friends and relatives that this training has, as its primary aim, safety in climbing. Only a fool really gets his kicks out of risking his life, and most climbers are not fools.

Well, then, what are they? They seem full of paradoxes. They are sometimes "loners," and are certainly individualists who shudder at the thought of regimentation. However, they readily accept teamwork, and gather in organized or unorganized groups for companionship. Climbing requires an unusual amount of physical fitness and stamina; yet many climbers are students or professional men. The sport demands serious attention to inherent hazard; yet climbers are humorous and lighthearted. Some are world-famous in the climbing fraternity for their skills and accomplishments; others have the capacity or desire to do only moderate climbs, but may enjoy the sport just as much.

Climbers are not of uniform build, age, or sex. The majority are young men in their late teens and early twenties, with a background of outdoor pursuits in which skills adaptable to climbing have been developed. Some start climbing later in life. Quite a few women and girls climb. Though they seldom have the strength or desire to be rope leaders, they take their place as team members with the same joys and obligations as their male companions. Technical climbing is not a sport for children or for very young teen-agers. They have neither the sustained interest nor the endurance necessary, and cannot take a responsible place on a rope until they reach fuller physical development and possess mature good judgment.

A climber's role in his sport does not remain static. An enthusiastic and talented beginner learns rapidly. Many climb fanatically for a few years and then quit. Others find climbing such an absorbing way of life that they pursue it for as long as physical capacities and time permit; experience, and often endurance, increase with the years. A snow and ice climber may add rock climbing to his repertoire, and a rock specialist may decide his forte is mountaineering.

People seldom climb half-heartedly. Most are simply unaware of the sport; some are intellectually intrigued but have no intention of becoming involved; others are horrified. But a few are wild about it. Why do they like to climb? Mountain climbing is a varied and challenging sport with great esthetic and physical appeal. Each climb is an adventure of such a highly personal nature that if you need to ask "Why?", you will never get an answer you fully understand. Climbers seldom try to explain their motivation to non-climbers, though they speculate and philosophize among themselves.

To each potential climber, the sport is an exciting new world. If it catches your interest, you have an inkling of *why*. If you want to know *how*, learn—but learn safely.

chapter two

Rock Climbing
For Beginners

A POOR but not uncommon way to start rock climbing is to go off with an equally inexperienced friend and an old rope, and try to work out protective techniques on your own. The best way is to climb with experienced, competent companions who have the advantage of several years' accumulated knowledge in modern techniques. Get instruction on the cliffs from those who know how.

Who Teaches Rock Climbing?

The first problem is to find knowledgeable companions who are willing to help you through the early stages of gaining experience. They may turn up by lucky chance; more likely, you will have to go out and hunt for them.

You can hang around groups of climbers in popular climbing areas, ask questions and exude interest and admiration until information and assistance are offered. Climbers are easily identified by their clanking equipment, coils of rope, and specialized footgear—not to mention their rock-worn garb and air of physical fitness. Professional guides and climbing schools are available in several major climbing areas (for a price, of course). Some colleges offer climbing and mountaineering courses. Or you can look up a climbing club in your school or geographical area. Some specialize in climbing only; some are sections of general outdoor clubs. Each group has its own regulations and methods. All offer opportunities for beginners to learn. Equally important, the members are available later as companions on the many and varied climbs that go into making a skilled climber. Much can be learned from books, but reading is no substitute for actual climbing.

Ground Work

If determined, you will find yourself among climbers willing and able to teach you. Your mentor may happen to be the type to take you at once on a long climb, where by necessity you quickly find out something about everything. It is more probable that you will spend hours on or near the ground, learning the basic techniques of safe climbing.

As an utter novice, you need not worry about providing equipment. Wear old clothes adequate for the weather, and rubber-soled shoes. The group or individual instructing provides the ropes. Though learners are expected to use the ropes, the owners are fussy about their lifelines, which must be treated with tender loving care: never stepped on, nor pulled needlessly in the dirt, nor dragged over sharp edges.

Knots

The protective use of the rope naturally involves tying your-self onto it. Knots used by climbers must be bombproof, fool-proof, correctly and quickly tied, and of a kind that can also be untied readily (without benefit of a hatchet). Practice the knots at home, with a piece of string or rope, until you can tie them under any conditions, no matter how adverse. The basic climbing knots, illustrated in the first seven figures of Chapter 2 (Figures 2-1 through 2-7), are drawn as they will look while you are tying them. Left-handed people often pre-fer to tie them in reverse.

Bowline

For tying the end of the rope around your waist. Standard-ize your method of tying it. For the version illustrated in Figure 2-1, pass the rope behind you from left to right. Now hold the long or "standing" part of the rope in your left hand, and the short end in your right. With the left hand, make a loop as shown. Put the end up through the loop, around the standing end, and back down through the loop. After tying the knot, work it along the rope until the waist loop is really snug. Test and set this knot with a good tug. The bowline tends to loosen with use, and should be safeguarded in one of the two ways illustrated in Figure 2-2: (1) Add one or two overhand knots around the waist loop. (2) Thread the end back through the knot before setting it. This is a less bulky method used by some experienced climbers. The end goes *over* the right side of the waist loop; *under* the left side; and up through the loop, parallel with the standing end. Several inches of rope should remain after the knot is secured; other-

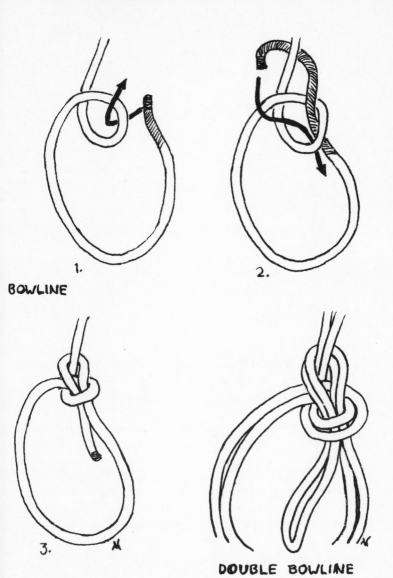

BOWLINE

1.

2.

3.

DOUBLE BOWLINE

Figure 2-1

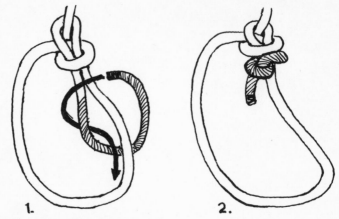

OVERHAND KNOT (SECURING BOWLINE)

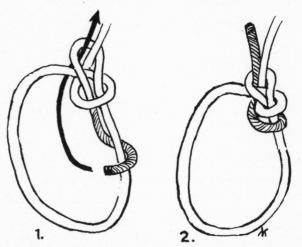

BOWLINE SECURED BY THREADING END THROUGH

Figure 2-2

wise retie the knot. Check the bowline occasionally during a climb and tighten the waist loop as necessary.

Bowline-on-a-Coil

Almost identical to the simple bowline, but more complicated to tie. Wind the rope around your waist several times, an arrangement which is more comfortable if you fall or must be held on the rope. Tie the knot around the coil as illustrated in Figure 2-3, and secure it.

Butterfly

Usually used for the middle man in rock climbing, when three people are tied into one rope. It is a symmetrical knot which is equally strong when pulled from either side. Make sure the waist loop is tightened before starting to climb. This knot tends to tighten in use, and is not secured (see Fig. 2-4).

Overhand

Used to prevent many other knots from slipping (see Fig. 2-2).

Water Knot

Used for joining ends of flat sling material. Tie an overhand knot, and thread the other end through it in the opposite direction, as shown in Figure 2-5. Make sure the two parts of the sling lie flat against each other throughout the knot.

Flemish Bend

Used to join two ropes of the same or unequal diameters.

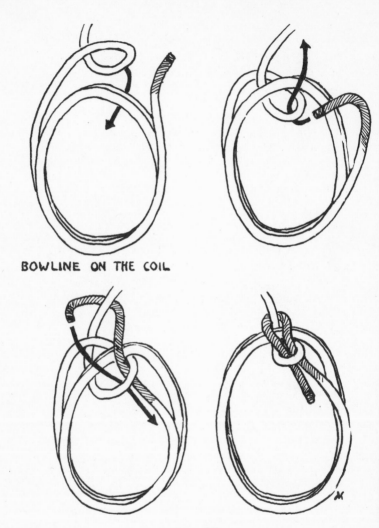

BOWLINE ON THE COIL

Figure 2-3

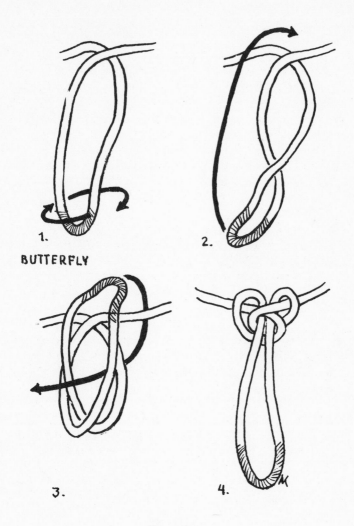

BUTTERFLY

1.

2.

3.

4.

Figure 2-4

It is similar to the water knot, but start by tying a figure-8 knot in one of the ends, leaving an ample end for a safety knot. Thread an end of the other rope through the knot in the opposite direction, as shown in Figure 2-6. The standing parts of the ropes pull against each other. Make sure the two ropes lie parallel throughout the entire knot. Tighten and test by pulling hard on the standing ends of both ropes, especially when the diameters are unequal. Secure on each side with one or more overhand knots.

Prusik

Formed by twisting a loop of light rope around a fixed rope hanging vertically, as illustrated in Figure 2-7. The prusik knot has the property of remaining in place when weighted, but slipping easily up or down when unweighted. This makes it possible to stand in loops, and ascend a rope in an emergency. The average person is physically unable to climb a long rope hand over hand; also, if you use your climbing rope for handholds, slack accumulates below, and you are no longer protected with an upper belay (see Upper Belays, later in this chapter). Prusik slings vary in size to fit the person. They should be approximately six feet in circumference, made from quarter-inch rope. Manila holds best, but nylon will serve if the sling is passed around the rope a third time. Even flat slings will work, but require more effort.

One of the standard techniques for ascending a rope with prusiks is to use three slings. Attached at intervals to the vertical rope, these form a chest loop for balance, and two footsteps. To ascend, stand with all your weight in the lowest sling, while raising the next one as high as you can step.

1. (OVERHAND KNOT)

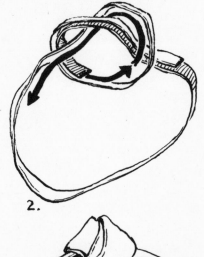

2.

3.

WATER KNOT (TIED IN WEBBING)

Figure 2-5

1.(FIGURE-8 KNOT)

2.

3.

FLEMISH BEND

Figure 2-6

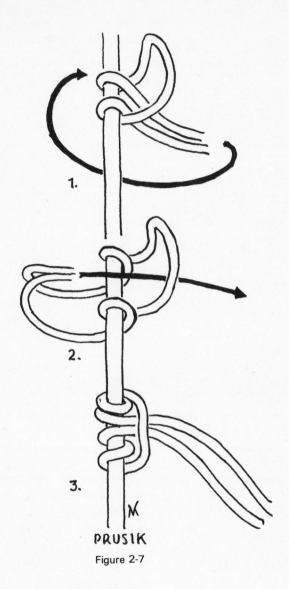

1.

2.

3.

PRUSIK

Figure 2-7

Transfer your weight to the upper footstep, and raise the chest loop as high as you can. Next pull up the rope below so you can reach the second foot loop, and slip it up as far as possible. Stand in both loops. Repeat. Prusiking can be practiced from the limb of a tree. The average prusik on rock is easier, as you are less apt to twirl around.

Other Knots

Variations of these knots, or different knots, are also employed, depending on the group or individual preference; or by experienced rock climbers for special situations.

Climbing with the Protection of the Rope

Once tied on, you can climb, with someone on the rocks above belaying as a safeguard in case you fall. The rope is intended as a protective device only. It is never used as a handhold, or to pull the climber up, except in specific types of advanced rock climbing (or desperation). The actual ascent of a cliff somewhat resembles climbing a very steep staircase, with scanty irregular treads, some wide and some narrow, at strange angles. The climber's legs normally do most of the work, with the hands and arms providing balance and any necessary upward pull. Avoid use of the knees; feet are more effective.

The key to an effortless ascent is balance, the knack of keeping the body weight over the feet, and away from the rock, at exactly the most efficient angle to make full use of whatever support the holds provide. There are many moves in rock climbing where no single hold can support you, but where perfect balance between several holds gives adequate purchase while you move rhythmically upwards. Such balance climbing is a muscle skill. If you are a "natural," you already possess this exquisite talent. But you may have to practice and cultivate the art.

Friction climbing is an example of pure balance climbing; the resistance between boot sole and rock is all that keeps you from slipping off, and momentum may permit progress where you cannot stand still. Types of special moves include the mantel, in which you push yourself up on a ledge with the heel of the hand or hands, as in getting out of a swimming pool; chimneying, in which various pressures of back, arms, and feet against opposing walls enable you to wiggle, or struggle, upwards; and the layback or lieback, in which the feet walk up the face of a cliff, held there by the pressure of the hands and arms pulling outward from a parallel crack, or from a flake that is sufficiently separated from the cliff to allow the fingers a grip behind it (very strenuous).

Upper Belays

The climbing maneuvers described, and others, can be performed with safety because the rope you are tied to is being taken in from above at the same rate you are climbing. An absolutely necessary step in learning roped climbing is acquiring the skill to protect other climbers. When giving an upper belay, you can easily hold the weight of a heavier person below.

First, sit down in a good spot, feet apart and braced firmly. As a beginner, you must be anchored (tied) to a rock, tree, piton, or even another climber, so you cannot be pulled off. The rope coming up from the climber below is passed around your hips. Both hands hold the rope, one on each side of your body, as illustrated in Figure 2-8. The hand on the climber's end guides, feels, and pulls in the rope. The other hand, on the opposite side of your body, holds the weight in case of a fall; the friction of the rope around the hips makes this surprisingly easy. Take the rope in by moving the feeling hand, which is pulling up the rope, toward the body, and extending the belay hand, also pulling the rope, away from the body; quickly slide both hands along the rope to their former positions; repeat. The belay hand must *never* leave the rope. While you are learning to belay, the climber below will call "Testing" before he starts to climb. Reply "Test!" and he will give a good pull, with his weight off the ground, so you can gain an idea of how it would feel if he fell off.

Learning to Handle the Rope

While belaying, you must watch the rope attentively. Lay the part you pull up in a compact pile (preferably within reach, and in a place where it is unlikely to snag on anything, or knock rocks down on the climber). Keep it taut between you and the climber, but do not jerk or pull. Your guiding hand on the rope informs you of how fast to take in rope; it is not unlike flying a kite or playing a fish.

The person climbing also has a responsibility toward the rope. He must keep it free of kinks, and make sure he does not overclimb the rope. If slack accumulates, he should slow down or stop until the rope is again taut. He must also watch the rope above him to make sure it has not caught on rocks or in cracks.

Climbing Signals

Climbers are frequently out of each other's sight, and may be almost out of earshot as well. Yet it is essential that each know what the other is doing. A set of verbal signals has been pretty well standardized among climbers; but in a new climbing group, check out what signals are used. Routine signals in roped climbing are:

Climber: "Belay on?"
Belayer: "Belay on."
Climber: "Ready to climb."
Belayer: "Climb!"
Climber: "Climbing."

Climber, if he wants the belayer to take in more rope, or take it in faster: "Rope!" or "Up rope!"

Climber, if he needs a lessening of tension, or extra slack for maneuvering, descending, throwing the rope, etc.: "Slack!"

Climber, to warn belayer: "Prepare for fall," or "Falling!"

Either, if a rock is dislodged: "Rock!"

Climber, when he is in a safe position near the belayer: "Belay off."

Belayer: "Belay off."

Except for "rope" and "slack," signals are usually repeated by the person they are meant for, as confirmation that he has heard, understood, and is taking action. You may have to shout repeatedly as loudly as possible, but do not assume the signal has been heard until you get an answer.

Learning to Rappel

Climbers have developed a method of descending steep rocks by sliding down a rope which is doubled around a fixed point. This is called rappelling or roping down. Meth-

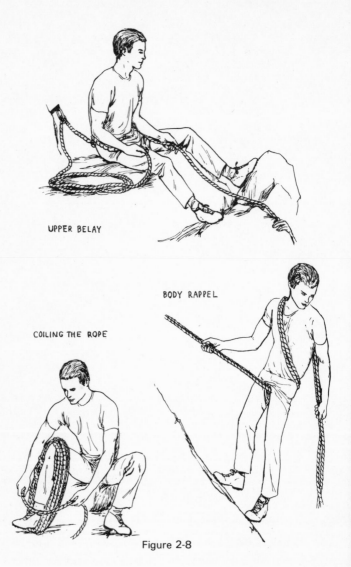

UPPER BELAY

COILING THE ROPE

BODY RAPPEL

Figure 2-8

ods and safety precautions used in affixing the rappel rope are explained in detail in Chapter Three.

As a neophyte, you begin with a simple body rappel, sometimes called the Dülfersitz, with a belay for safety. To get into the rappel, stand below the point where the rope is fixed. Face the cliff and straddle the rope. Take hold of the doubled rope behind you, and bring it forward across the left hip. Pull it up *across* your chest, and backwards over your right shoulder. The doubled rope now hangs down behind you. Grasp it with the left (lower) hand, palm forward and thumb downward, as illustrated in Figure 2-8. This hand supports your weight, holds you into the rope, and must *never* let go. The right hand holds the rope above you for balance; if you need a spare hand, use the upper one. A left-handed person may feel better with the whole arrangement reversed.

Now lean backwards in the rope. Your body should be at about a 45-degree angle to the rock, knees bent slightly, and feet 24 to 36 inches apart for balance on the varying inclines. Looking down over your left shoulder to see where you are going, walk backwards or sideways down the cliff. The rope slides slowly through your hands and over your body. The points of greatest friction, hip and opposite shoulder, become very evident if you go too fast. For a long rappel, extra padding is needed at these points to avoid a rope burn. The lower hand controls the speed of descent; nothing is gained by gripping frantically with the upper hand. At the bottom, step out of the rope, and call "Off rappel" to those above.

Coiling the Rope

One of the beginner's duties is to learn how to coil the climbing rope for carrying and storage. Methods vary. A good one is illustrated in Figure 2-8. Sit down and cock one knee so your foot rests on the heel. Wind a length of rope around knee and foot. Tie a square knot, leaving an end about fifteen inches long. Wind the rope firmly into a coil around foot and knee. Wrap the last ten feet or so around and around the coil to hold it together. The two ends of the rope are joined with a square knot.

Personal Climbing Equipment

Soon after your climbing begins, some personal climbing equipment is needed. Notice what your companions are using, and ask their advice. Go slow about acquiring equipment until you know what you really want and need. Many sporting goods stores handle, or specialize in, mountaineering supplies. There are also excellent mail order sources of mountaineering equipment which publish very informative catalogues. If you become seriously interested in rock climbing, you should have the following minimum of personal equipment:

Kletterschuhe

Specialized rock climbing shoes from Europe, usually of grey suede, with thin black lug soles, often without heels. They should fit snugly over one pair of light socks, to provide a good feel and grip on rock. European sizes have been loosely translated into American sizes, and do not run true.

Piton Hammer

Needed by any rock climber who gets off the ground in

rope work. Its main function is to drive and remove pitons. A ball-peen hammer is satisfactory to start with, until you know exactly the kind you want to buy. Piton hammers of both American and European make are available in a wide price range. The head is square, and has a wedge or point at the other end, as shown in Figure 2-9. Choose one that feels balanced in your hand and is heavy enough for a real wallop.

The hammer must be fitted with a sling to guard against being dropped. Piton hammers come with a hole in the handle (if using a ball-peen hammer, drill a hole). Thread it with a length of nylon cord tied in a loop that goes around your neck and one arm. The completed sling should be as long as your greatest reach with either hand. The hammer is usually carried in a belt holster (occasionally in a hip pocket).

Pitons

Metal spikes with an eye or ring in the head, especially made from various alloys, to be driven into rock cracks of many different sizes, shapes, depths, and configurations. Experienced climbers always have a large variety of pitons (sometimes called "pins"). Several common types are illustrated in Figure 2-9. The beginner needs only a few. Choose three or four horizontals and one or two angles. Your future needs will depend on the difficulty and location of your climbs. For the present, practice driving pitons into cracks for belay anchors.

Carabiners

Steel or aluminum alloy snaplinks, about four inches long, with a spring gate-opening. Carabiners are most commonly

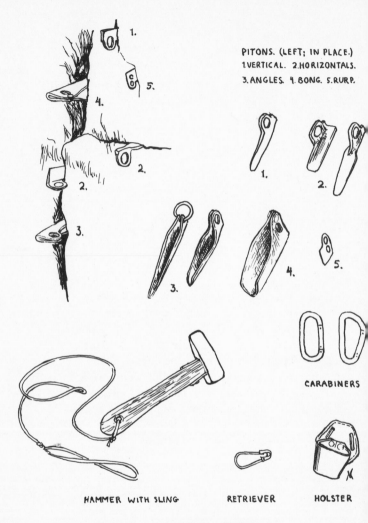

PITONS. (LEFT; IN PLACE.)
1.VERTICAL. 2.HORIZONTALS.
3.ANGLES. 4. BONG. 5.RURP.

CARABINERS

HAMMER WITH SLING   RETRIEVER   HOLSTER

ROCK CLIMBING EQUIPMENT
Figure 2-9

oval; others are pear- or "D"-shaped, etc. Carabiners are used to connect the climbing rope with the eye of the piton; also for carrying pitons, rigging slings, and many other purposes. Start with a minimum of four.

Piton Keeper or Retriever

A lightweight clip, fastened to your person with a light cord, to prevent loss of pitons while driving or removing them. Very useful to beginners, who are regrettably subject to dropping other people's pitons, but rarely used by advanced climbers.

Slings

Loops, varying from about three to twelve feet in circumference. They may be bought ready-made, or constructed from quarter-inch rope or from flat nylon webbing one-half to one inch wide. All nylon rope and sling material, when cut, should immediately have the ends lightly fused with a match or other flame to prevent raveling. To make the loop in rope, tie the ends with a Flemish bend and overhand knots. In webbing, use a water knot, and sew the ends back flat to the loop, by hand or sewing machine. You should always carry a few assorted slings for various uses.

Rucksack

A small summit pack is needed to keep your stuff together, and transport it to the start of the climb. It is also needed on the actual climb, and the least experienced member of the party often has the honor of carrying everyone's supplies.

Consecutive Climbing on Multi-Pitch Routes

Having practiced the basic techniques and acquired some equipment, you are ready for multi-pitch rock climbing. A pitch is the distance climbed between belay spots.

Routes

Climbs are not made anywhere on a cliff, at random. The route goes up a portion of cliff broken by natural forces into connecting cracks, ledges, chimneys, flakes, etc., which provide handholds and footholds, piton cracks and belay stances. Routes viewed from a distance may appear very steep, but a side view usually reveals them to have an easier angle than is apparent head on. Usually you find more holds when you are climbing than there appeared to be from a distance (though the opposite may also be true). Climbs you are doing generally seem quite unsensational compared with ones you may have watched.

Climbing Parties

A "rope" means not only the object itself, but also the team that climbs tied together. The usual number on a rope is two or three. As a beginner, you will probably start consecutive climbing as third, at the end of a three-man rope, and can learn what is involved without much additional responsibility. After the rope is made up, the climbers go to the foot of the chosen route. They may scramble some distance up the base of the cliffs without roping up. Never hesitate to ask for a belay if you feel insecure at this stage. The climbing ropes are uncoiled, hammers and hardware adjusted, and the climbers rope up.

Order of Climbing

The second man takes his belay position, and the leader climbs. He may place pitons from time to time. When he reaches the next belay spot, he stops, prepares to belay, and calls to the second to climb. You, as the third man, have so far done nothing. When the second starts to climb, watch the rope going up to him, make sure it does not snag, and perhaps pay it out. When the second reaches the leader, he takes up his belay stance, and the leader climbs another pitch. You, the third man, are again doing nothing; but be ready to climb as soon as the word comes down—and do not forget the rucksack.

When the leader is at the top of the second pitch, the second man turns his attention to the third and last man. If there is extra rope between you, he will pull it up; you should notify him when it is all taken up. Signals are exchanged, and you start to climb. If you reach a piton, you will see that the rope is running through a carabiner snapped into the piton's eye. Stop in as convenient a position as possible, remove the rope from the carabiner, snap the carabiner out of the piton, and secure it in your waist loop, or on a sling carried for the purpose (do not trust your belt).

Next remove the piton. Hammer it forcefully as far as it will go to one side, and then all the way to the other side, back and forth until it can be pulled out with your fingers. Your position may be precarious or uncomfortable; if it is too tiring, call "Tension!" and the belayer will support you on the rope while you work. When the piton begins to loosen up, snap your keeper into its eye so it will not pop out and go clanging down the cliff. If a keeper is not available, you can use a carabiner and sling, but avoid battering the 'biner. Pitons can be stubborn, but most do come out with time, persistence, and might. If your stop has been a long one, call out "Climbing!" to let your belayer know you are moving again. When you reach the second man, you may find that he is anchored with a sling or with a section of the climbing rope to a rock, tree, or piton. Tie yourself on in the same way. Hand the hardware you have collected to the second, who takes it along for the leader's use.

Be attentive to your rope mates' needs and instructions. Do not climb until you receive the signal to do so. Watch and tend the rope. Once on the climb, you may as well belay the second: it is good practice for learning to handle the rope adeptly, and an extra safeguard for the entire party. Remember to remove the anchor piton, etc., before starting the next pitch.

Tips for Beginners

A few pointers may help you, as the beginner on your first long climbs. Concentrate on the climbing. Watch the climbers ahead of you, as it is helpful to know which holds they use and how, even though you may climb the pitch differently. If you cannot get going with one set of holds, try another combination. Make use of small holds close together to minimize the effort of hauling yourself up. Climb quickly. Many holds are fine for a swift, smooth passage, but not as a stopping place. Rests should be made on large holds.

A few cautions are also in order. You will probably be too busy to notice the empty spaces beneath you, known in climbing parlance as "exposure." Or you may find the sight wonderfully exhilarating. But if it scares you, look back at the rock and rope, and remember that you are well protected. (You are almost sure to become fond of exposure, or at least inured to it, as your techniques improve.) Check your waist loop occasionally. Be very careful not to dislodge rocks with feet or rope, and test handholds that might come off. If a rock does fall, yell "Rock! Rock!" for the benefit of anyone below. If you see or hear one coming from above, get your head up against the rock, into a crack, or under an overhang. If you cannot take cover, watch the rock and duck at the last minute. Whenever possible, keep out from under climbers above. Even if the climbing gets hairy and the pitons won't budge, refrain from complaint. Grunt, ask advice, or make jokes—but don't claim you "can't." Don't talk too much; it distracts your companions and sometimes annoys them. Listen to the more experienced; there is still much to learn.

chapter three

Gaining Experience
On Rock

HAVING mastered the basic techniques of rock climbing and tried a multi-pitch ascent, you have reached a sort of crossroads. Some beginners, of course, decide the sport is not for them, though its elementary safety measures may prove useful on non-technical climbs. Others, swept away by the sheer delight of rock climbing, are affected as if a sort of revelation has changed their entire outlook on life. It has.

The Advanced Beginner and Intermediate Climber

If you are among the converts, your beginner's role as passive third on the rope will not last long. With the basic know-how, you will probably begin to belay the leader on easy climbs. In due time, depending on your ability, temperament, and enthusiasm, you will start leading. It is well to make your initial leads on familiar climbs that were easy for you, and to have an experienced second man. By this time, too, additional equipment, and a full familiarity with its uses for protection, are required.

Expert techniques and good judgment are best developed during a period in which you are a sort of apprentice or understudy, making diverse climbs with many climbers. You should progress from easy to difficult climbs at your own tempo; but it will take at least one or two climbing seasons, perhaps several or many, before you reach your top potential as a climber. Whether you turn out to be an average or an outstanding rock climber remains to be seen—and has little correlation with your enjoyment of the sport. In any event, both ascent and descent are more complex than they seem from the comparatively carefree tail end of the rope.

Number of Climbers on a Rope

A roped climbing party routinely is made up of either two or three people, preferably two on rock. More than three is such a time-consuming and cumbersome number that it can be justified only by an emergency. For instance, when two ropes are on the same route, the parties occasionally join because of unexpected climbing difficulties, storm, or indisposition.

The Three-Man Rope

A rope of three may be chosen for reasons such as companionship, extra safety on some climbs, photography, instruction, or shortage of rope leaders. The third man, of course, is not necessarily inexperienced. He may be an alternate leader who swings leads with the fellow at the other end. The least experienced person may have been tied into the middle for extra protection on a traverse. In such cases, the usual climbing order is changed: the third joins the others at each belay stance to take his turn at leading, or to belay the leader if the second is a beginner.

Three climbers may tie into a 150-foot rope. If such a rope is not available, or if the climb requires long leads, two shorter ropes are used. The middle man ties into the end of the rope that goes to the leader, leaving an end about thirty inches long which is joined to the second rope. The knot should be within a few inches of his body; thus it cannot interfere when carabiners are reached.

The Two-Man Rope

Two on a rope climb about twice as fast as three. There is less rope handling and general maneuvering. Speed is not, of course, the primary aim of climbing; but it is essential on long or difficult routes, and smooth, fast climbing is sheer pleasure.

On two-man ropes, the order of climbing may take two forms. (1) The two climbers may be of equal or nearly equal ability. Since both want to lead, they take turns on alternate pitches; or, one may be an intermediate climber who leads the less difficult sections. In either case, the leader brings the second up to his ledge. There the second adds whatever hardware he needs from the belayer's assortment to his own supply. He then leads the next pitch. Besides giving both climbers a chance to lead, this procedure minimizes transfer of hardware, changing belay positions, and rope handling.

(2) The two may be climbers of unequal abilities, or two who form an almost permanent team that almost always climbs together with one leading and the other second. An example of such a rope is a husband-wife team, in which the woman usually climbs second.

On two-man ropes, the second performs all the functions of the third, as well as those specifically the obligation of the second man, whose primary activity is belaying the leader.

Relationship Between Rope Leader and Second Man

Both the rope leader and the second man should have a thorough understanding of each other's duties and responsibilities in order to climb as a team with the greatest safety, efficiency and pleasure.

Generally the rope leader has served a stint as second while gaining the climbing experience and personal insight needed for competent leading. Sometimes he is a climber of such agility, drive, and daring that he never spent much time as second-man "apprentice" climber. However, every leader at least occasionally climbs as second with his peers, and hence not only can fulfill the functions of second man, but also knows how far he must and can trust his second.

The second man may be a climber of such knowledge, dependability, and competence that, whether he leads or not, he knows exactly what the leader is doing, and how to coordinate his own efforts. Or he may be a climber of limited experience who does not yet possess the self-confidence, desire, or ability to lead. He may fit somewhere in between.

Leader's Responsibilities

The word "leader" commonly has two connotations. The term may refer to a climber with sufficient experience and judgment to take charge of a group, regardless of whether he goes first on the rope. It may also refer to the rope leader, whether or not he is qualified to make decisions for the group. Actually leaders usually fall into both categories. When they don't, the distinction is perfectly clear on a climb. The leader's position is one of challenge, and of risks that do not ordinarily apply to his followers. He also has duties and responsibilities, which include a knowledge of what he himself as well as others can climb safely.

Selecting the Route

In choosing a route, the leader should consider the whole party's abilities and desires. If he picks a route too hard for the party, the climb may turn into one long session of coaxing and cajoling, or a retreat. True, many neophytes can climb much harder things than they think they can; but also true, only the really dedicated are encouraged by discovering this the hard way. The rope leader also has to figure out move by move which holds, cracks, faces, gullies, ridges and ledges will "go." The leader's route-finding ability improves with experience, first on known and then on unfamiliar routes.

Equipment for the Climb

The leader should know, or find out, enough about the prospective climb to choose the needed equipment. Previous knowledge, friends' advice, or a guidebook will indicate the length, difficulty, and nature of the route—all of which influence what ropes, slings, and hardware should be taken. Extra gear is usually provided in case poor weather or other unpredictable conditions should make the climb harder than expected. Necessary food, water, and clothing should be included. Every member of the rope should have a piton hammer on his person, plus a couple of slings and at least one piton and carabiner.

Unique Problems of the Climbing Leader

The most obvious difference between the leader and those following on the rope is that he lacks the almost perfect protection of an upper belay. He climbs with the rope below him. The rope itself creates quite a downward pull, especially when friction is greatly increased by corners of rock, carabiners, etc. Further, it may catch, or the belayer may fail to pay it out properly and thereby cause a downward jerk. The major hazard is that if the leader falls at all, he will, if unprotected, fall at least twice the distance between his stance and his belayer.

It is quite true that the born leader glories in the exultation and the challenge of what he is doing. But he also prides himself on his competence, which includes safe climbing. He gets used to the pull of the rope and compensates for it. He adapts his climbing to the abilities of the second. And he makes use of pitons or similarly employed protective devices to prevent too long a fall.

Use of Equipment for Leader Protection

Every reliable climbing leader gets a feel for what he can

climb without falling. Considerable experience on a variety of climbs cultivates this feel. When the rock above looks as if a fall might occur—and preferably before his position gets really shaky—the leader looks for a suitable crack, if possible one above him. He drives a piton into the crack, snaps a carabiner into it, and snaps the rope into the carabiner. He is now protected to the extent that if he is below his piton, he is essentially as well protected as if he had a standard upper belay. When he has climbed above the piton, he can theoretically fall only twice the distance between himself and the piton. The principle of piton protection is shown in Figure 3-1.

After placing his first piton of the pitch, the leader should signal to his belayer to make sure he is aware that the pull will now come up instead of down. The belayer should also be notified of additional protection placed (unless, of course, he can plainly see or hear the procedure), so he can take it into account in belaying. Other protective devices used by the leader with the same effect as pitons are bolts, slings, and nuts for special circumstances. These are discussed later in this chapter, under Choosing and Caring for Equipment.

When to Place Pitons

The need for a piton depends largely on the relationship between the climber's experience and ability, and the difficulty of the route. As a beginning leader, you may place them at six-foot intervals along the entire route if you so desire; but when you find out how much time and energy are required, you probably won't want to. Nonetheless, while

LEADER FALL WITH
PITON PROTECTION

SECOND MAN
BELAYING LEADER

Figure 3-1

learning, you should use more protection than a more experienced climber. It is a most appropriate safeguard.

The size and experience of the belayer are also considered. The more pitons, the more friction, and the more effortlessly a fall can be held. The probable landing place if you fall, and the type of fall that might occur, also influence the location and number of pitons placed. A fall into a rather gentle trough or onto a ledge would not place as great stress on the piton as a free fall, but the climber is more likely to be injured if he strikes something than if the fall is free. Try to place pitons so solid landings are avoided. On traverses, pitons afford both the leader and the last on the rope protection from long, swinging pendulum falls. Do not feel limited to using pitons only where previous climbers did; use more (or less) if you feel like it.

How and Where to Place Pitons

Driving pitons is a craft, a skill, an art, on which the climber's life may hang. In a piton fall, the shock of the falling man hits the man himself, the rope, the carabiner, the piton, and the belayer almost simultaneously. The force exerted on the piton and carabiner is twice the force of the fall itself, since it is the sum of both the fall and the belay that stops it. A poorly placed piton may be jerked violently from its crack and alter the entire sequence of protection (for the worse). As in other aspects of technical climbing, much experience is necessary to achieve expertise in piton-craft; but a few pointers will help the beginner begin.

Reduced to its simplest and most ideal conditions, the

method of placing a piton when need arises consists in first finding a properly located crack that appears to narrow gradually for several inches behind its opening. Pick a crack to fit one of your pitons, or more likely a piton to fit the crack. Horizontal pitons (which have the eyes set at right angles to the blades) can be used in any thin cracks. Vertical (flat) pitons are less versatile (and may not even be carried). They are suitable only for narrow cracks that do not have offset edges, and that slope no more than thirty degrees from the probable direction of fall. Wider cracks require angles, and still larger openings take bongs. Various pitons in place are illustrated in Figure 2-9.

The eye of the piton should be downward unless an offset, bulge, etc., prevents. Angles and bongs should have the open side downward in horizontal cracks, and sideways in vertical cracks. Select a piton of such thickness that preferably three-quarters (and not less than half) of the blade length can enter the crack before driving. Soft rock requires long pitons. While driving, listen to each hammer blow. If the rock is good, and crack and piton compatible, each blow will ring on the piton with an increasingly high pitch; a dull, hollow sound often indicates a poor piton. The piton should go in hard, and if possible up to the eye (leaving enough room to insert the carabiner). Pitons *must* be sound. Secondarily, they should not be overdriven, for removal becomes time-consuming and often impossible. Test with a medium blow in each direction, parallel to the crack. If the piton is questionable, clip in carabiner and rope, and test it further by jerking on the rope from a safe spot.

Of course, actual conditions are not always ideal. Either piton or crack may have been misjudged. If the piton goes in too easily or sticks out so far that a fall might lever it out of its crack, remove it and try it in another spot, or use it for temporary protection while a different piton is placed elsewhere.

If your position makes it imperative to hold on with one hand, place your piton with the other. Until you become adept, attach your retriever to the eye of the piton to prevent dropping it, stick it in the crack, and gingerly let go. Start hammering with the gentlest of taps. If it falls out, try again. The retriever can be removed when the piton is well started. Try to position a series of pitons in a reasonably straight line to minimize rope friction.

The quality of the rock may preclude really good piton placement. Clean, sharply fractured granite is the prototype of perfect piton rock. Even here, be on the lookout for blocks or flakes, sometimes astonishingly big, that tend to move with the leverage of one or more pitons, the crack widening or an entire section coming loose. Decomposed granite, sandstone, brittle volcanic rock, shattered limestone, or other types of rock that do not fracture cleanly or are unsound, cause the prudent climber to regard his degree of protection with suspicion. However, determined and experienced climbers have devised methods of compensating for poor piton rock in several ways. They may nest a whole cluster of pitons in an unlikely little hole, place pitons very close together, treat them with inordinately gentle care, place a "hero loop" (short nylon sling) around a protruding piton close to the rock instead of through the eye, or employ various other types of protection. Such methods are best deferred until you have gained a good deal of experience.

Re-using Pitons

The last man on the rope removes the pitons, passing
them along to the leader. This is done for several reasons.
On long routes or remote climbs, the weight must be considered. Just the right piton might be needed several times
on the same route. Thrift enters in. Climbing ethics suggest
leaving the rocks in their natural state, and also requiring
other parties to place their own pitons.

Pitons are not always removed. On some routes frequently
climbed by club groups, pitons may be left in place to save
wear and tear either on the cracks or on beginning leaders.
In such cases, repress your joy at "finding" a piton to add to
your collection, and leave it in. However, pitons are often
left either because they would not come out, or the last man
lacked the strength, will, and persistence to get them out;
these are fair pickings. Pitons found in place should never be
used for protection without testing them. They frequently
become unsafe or loose from corrosion of the metal or because the crack has widened due to various natural factors
such as freezing of water, cyclic temperature changes, and
the like. At times, two ropes are on the same route, and by
pre-arrangement the first rope may leave the pitons in place
to save time or to assist a less experienced rope; the last man
on the second rope takes them out and passes them up to the
first rope.

Carabiner Handling

The use of carabiners is much less complicated than that
of pitons. Usually the carabiner is hooked into the piton eye.
Then the rope is snapped into the carabiner. The easiest way

to put the carabiner into the piton eye is to hold it with the gate-opening up and towards the rock. Push the gate against the piton so the gate opens and the carabiner slips into the eye. Then invert the carabiner so the gate is outward from the rock and facing down, to prevent accidental opening against the rock.

Be sure the rope from below runs through the carabiner in a direction that will permit it to run free when you are above it. If a piton is placed in a deep recess, or well to one side, or in some other position that causes the rope to bind or pull over a sharp edge, make a chain with two or more carabiners or use a good sling as a link between two carabiners, to allow the rope to run more freely. Carabiners are useful in countless ways, but should not be used so lavishly that you run out of them before completing the pitch.

Rope Problems

In leading, the first man should keep an eye on the rope behind him, as the second often cannot see all the rope. If it catches in a crack or over a point, the leader should throw the rope to try to loosen it. Sometimes both first and second must work together on this. Toward the end of the pitch, the friction may become so great that the rope has to be hauled up a few feet before each move. Once out of sight of the second, keep him informed of your activities to aid in smooth rope handling. If you need temporary support on the rope, possible when it is running through a carabiner at your level or above, call "Tension!" If a fall seems imminent, warn the belayer.

Direct Aid

Pitches where the holds are scanty or lacking, but the cracks are good, may be ascended with the use of pitons, carabiners, and slings for aid and assistance. A long sling tied with two or three loops in it for footsteps may be linked by a carabiner to a high piton. Used occasionally on moderate climbs, such aid makes the climbs easier (and is avoided by most climbers for this very reason). Another type of aid involves the use of mechanical ascenders such as Jumars for climbing fixed ropes. Direct aid, used extensively on very high-angle climbs, is an advanced and specialized technique for such routes as sheer, almost holdless walls. Leaders and seconds tend to work up gradually to this sort of thing.

The Second Man

The rope, pitons, and carabiners are useless in team climbing without the skills of the second man. The leader relies upon his second to respond quickly and properly to his needs and signals, to handle the rope smoothly and expertly, and to catch him in case he falls either with or without pitons in place. The second has an assortment of duties, of which by far the most important is safeguarding the leader. For this responsibility, he should be prepared by instruction and practice. Figure 3-1 shows the second giving one type of belay for holding a leader fall, and will clarify the following discussion.

Types of Leader Falls

There are two distinct types of leader falls: (1) From above, without pitons or similar protective devices in place. Techniques for holding the fall are variations on those used in an ordinary upper belay to allow for the much greater jolt. (2) From above, after a piton or sling is in place and the rope connected to it with a carabiner. The essential difference to the belayer is that he receives an upward, rather than a downward, jerk. This type of fall is known as a "piton fall."

Practice in Belaying the Leader

In spite of all the effort going into protection, leaders seldom fall off in actual climbing. You may go through your entire climbing career without once having to field a leader. However, if a fall comes, the demands on the belayer are so severe, and his reaction so important, that holding leader falls should be one of the techniques practiced diligently before it is actually needed. Otherwise, you can hardly conceive of the jolt you may get—or, surprisingly, how well you can hold the fall when you know how. Though you might succeed unrehearsed, it is one thing that you should not count on learning "as you go along."

Two or three people can practice the technique with simple setups such as a very sound piton and carabiner above an overhang, or from the lowest limb of a suitable tree. One climber, pretending to be a falling leader, can jump off while another tries to hold him. Unfortunately, the faller may be let down too far by an inexperienced belayer. A safer method (although in some respects more trouble) is to replace the climber with a dead weight, such as a log, a large tire, or a bucket of concrete that has a bent reinforcing bar embedded in it for attaching it to the rope. The object need not be as heavy as a man. For one thing, unlike a living body, it does not absorb part of the shock of the fall; and for another, more slack can be safely accumulated in the rope. This system is best used for a group or club, as several people are needed to haul the weight back up after each "fall." For practicing with a dead weight, use an old rope retired from active climbing.

The learning belayer must be positioned and anchored safely beyond the line of fall of the weight. Except for this precaution the techniques are much the same as on a climb.

Belay Stance of Second Man on Climb

In the selection of belay spots, there are several considerations. (1) Exposure to rock or leader fall. If there is any choice (and sometimes there is not), be to one side of the line of ascent, lest a dislodged rock or the climber himself put you out of commission by falling on you. (2) View of the leader. If possible, sit where you can watch the leader. This facilitates proper rope handling. When you can no longer see him, be especially attentive in listening for signals. (3) Direction of rope going up to leader. Pick a position from which the rope runs as directly as possible to the leader's proposed line of ascent. Ask him which way he intends to go, if it is not obvious. (4) Direction of possible leader fall. Consider carefully where he would fall, and how the force of the fall would come on you. If the force would be downward, try to sit or stand so the greatest force of the fall would be directly down between your well-braced legs. The direction of fall determines which will be the holding hand in the belay. If the fall would be to your right, the right hand should guide the rope and the left hand do the holding—and vice versa. Thus the friction of the body always intervenes between the fall and the holding hand. If the braking hand is unavoidably close to the cliff, holding it between your legs sometimes prevents its being jerked against the rock (in rock climbing, the skin over the knuckles is usually the first to go). The route may change direction so that the holding hand has to be switched to the opposite side, or the belay position altered. In either case, signals must be exchanged to indicate that the leader is momentarily in a spot where he can remain unbelayed while the change is made.

Anchoring the Belayer

For giving an upper belay, you frequently can find a good place to sit from which you couldn't be dislodged. For a leader belay, tie yourself on unless you have a very superior spot, such as a wide ledge with excellent bracing for the feet, or a tree or point of rock that can be straddled with passable comfort. Anchoring is especially advisable for a belayer who is small compared with the leader. If the leader was anchored while bringing you up, use his anchor point. Otherwise establish your own. Sometimes an anchor can be arranged by placing a sling around bush, tree, or point of rock, and fastening your waist loop to the sling with a carabiner. Often a piton has to be placed for an anchor. Drive it as low as possible, preferably close by and behind you. Put a carabiner in the piton and tie in, sometimes with a sling but usually with a section of the climbing rope. If the anchor point is within reach or close by, tie an overhand loop in a bight of the rope, and insert it in the carabiner. The anchor should be long enough so it is fairly taut, but allows you to sit comfortably. If the anchor point is farther away, place the rope leading from your waist through the carabiner; adjust the length of the anchor and tie a bight of the rope into your waist loop with one or two overhand knots. When the anchor piton is above, and particularly sound, the leader sometimes runs his climbing rope through the same carabiner to protect the belayer from the direct shock of a fall. Do not unanchor till the leader has called "Belay on!" from the next belay spot.

Position of Rope for Holding Leader Fall

For a downward pull, sit down if the belay spot permits. At times you have to belay from a place barely large enough for your feet, and you half-stand, half-lean against the cliff (well anchored, of course). If you think the belay rope could be jerked off your hips by a downward pull, place it above the anchor rope. Otherwise it is better to have it run under the anchor. After the leader has placed one piton, a fall might result in a very severe upward jerk on the belayer. An inexperienced belayer, or one small in size, may find it expeditious to place the belay rope under his buttocks in expectation of such a fall. If he is in a standing or half-standing position, he can essentially sit in the rope, ready to drop his full weight into it to take the initial shock. This position is often employed on practice climbs when a dead weight is to be held. However, most experienced belayers simply give the leader a belay around their hips or under their shoulders. The shock of the fall is usually lessened by the friction of the rope going through several carabiners; the force is seldom directly upward on a real climb, and this is the safest position to be in if the pitons come out. True, the rope might be jerked up under the armpits; some climbers lessen the possibility by running the belay rope through a carabiner in the waist loop when they are giving a leader belay around their hips.

Dynamic Belay

When the leader takes a long fall before the rope catches him, it often is held with the so-called dynamic (or running) belay. The instant the fall occurs, tighten your belay hand on the rope, and simultaneously bring the belaying hand across your body toward the opposite side to increase rope friction. As the force of the fall comes on you, the rope should run a little through your hands and over your body, and the person falling should be brought to a quick but not joltingly sudden stop. A "braking" stop is easier on every link of the protective chain, and on the falling climber. It is somewhat like braking a car to a fast stop, compared with an instantaneous stop caused by running into a wall.

The amount the rope should run depends on the length, force, and location of the fall. It also depends upon the type of rope in use. The standard nylon climbing rope is fairly elastic, but a long fall cannot and should not be held without the rope running a few feet while the friction caused by the belay and other factors stops it. With major changes in equipment, techniques often change, sometimes controversially. Some advanced rock specialists use the recently developed "dynamic ropes," which have so much built-in stretch that letting the rope run at all appears redundant.

Do not get the idea that *any* rope should run just for the

sake of running. The sole aim of the belay is to *stop the fall*. If the rope runs too far, the belayer may lose control of it or get severe rope burns on his hands; and the falling climber may strike a ledge or outcrop before he can be stopped. The technique of holding leader falls must be practiced diligently under the supervision of experienced climbers before it is ever needed.

Factors Influencing Severity of Leader Falls

A piton fall is not necessarily very severe or hard to hold. It varies with a number of quite predictable factors: (1) How far the leader falls. (2) Whether the fall is free or slowed by the friction of the man sliding along the rock. (3) How many carabiners the rope runs through; the more carabiners (especially if they are not in a straight line), the more friction. There is no rope-running when holding falls where the carabiner setup generates much friction.

Other Duties of the Second Man

Be sure the rope runs smoothly. While paying it out, allow a couple of feet of slack between you and the leader, so if he moves suddenly he won't get a jerk. If the rope has been laid in a loose pile (less apt to cause kinks than laying it in a coil as it is taken in), it usually goes up freely. But it is well known that ropes have a perverse will of their own about snarling and catching. Use your "feeling" hand to keep at least several feet of rope free of tangles. If one hand is insufficient, or you can't undo it fast enough, tell the leader to stop climbing while you straighten out the snarl.

Notify the leader as to the approximate amount of rope

left when he has quite a bit of it out; this gives him a clue as to when he must find the next belay spot. On difficult routes, you might tell him when the middle mark goes by; certainly you should start signaling when there are about thirty feet left (estimate; don't try to measure). The leader is now far away; call loudly, "Thirty feet," "Twenty feet," "Ten!"—and repeat until you have an answer. Be awfully emphatic when you get down to five; if there is *no* rope left, a dynamic belay is impossible. Occasionally a leader who has almost or just reached a belay stance with no rope to spare will request you to unanchor, or even move if you safely can, to give him a few feet more.

The second man, of course, removes the hardware and usually carries the pack if he is end man.

Special Problems of the Middle Man

If there is a third on the rope, the second man has additional functions. He alternately belays the leader and the third and has to keep the two climbing ropes separate. This problem is not acute unless all three persons are on the same spot, in which case the two ropes should be laid on separate piles (preferably one on each side of the middle man), and the other climbers should help in the rope handling. As middle man you may find yourself wound up a few times in both ropes unless you are careful to take off each belay the same way you put it on (over the head or over the feet). It's more confusing than amusing.

When climbing in the middle, you suffer the same drag of the rope behind you that the leader does (but at least you have an upper belay). When you come to a carabiner, take out the rope in front, and place the rope behind in the same carabiner—running in the same direction, too. This gives the third man a direct upper belay even if the route winds back and forth, and is particularly necessary on traverses. If friction is great and protection of the third man does not require the rope to go through all the carabiners, remove some of them. Mention it to the third so he won't overlook the pitons, or take the pitons out yourself.

Descending Multi-Pitch Climbs

What goes up must come down is a truism applicable to a happy climbing party assembled on top of cliff or spire. There are several modes of descent (not all possible choices for every climb).

Walking Down

Usually the easiest and fastest, if an easy way exists.

Climbing Down

Direct and quick on fairly easy climbs, either by the route of ascent or a different known route. Climbing down is also an excellent way to gain experience before it is forced upon you, as it is often more difficult than climbing up and requires somewhat different techniques. It is difficult to see where you are going and where to place the feet, and your anatomy is not so well suited to going down as up even though gravity is with you. Face outwards as long as you can; when necessary, turn sideways to use the holds and still watch for footholds; and when you get to steep places where you have to face the cliff to make use of the holds, combine feeling with your feet and occasional looks. In down-climbing, the leader goes last to protect the party. His second should place pitons *below* difficult spots for the leader's safety. The first person down should consult the others, if he has any doubt about the route.

Rappelling

Often the chosen method of descent. It is easy, and fun on steep cliffs free of loose rock. For absolute safety, many climbing groups recommend that all rappels be made with belays, or that at least the first man down be belayed. In reality, however, this is seldom done on actual climbs under good conditions. Often there is no spare rope available for a belay; the process is awkward and time-consuming; and too, a belay is of little use to the last man down. Rappel techniques should be learned with a belay. On climbs, rappel safety depends on everyone, regardless of experience, exercising extreme care at every stage of every rappel. An unbelayed rappel is perfectly safe *only as long as nothing goes wrong*. If something does go wrong, the results are usually fatal. Many phases of rappelling on cliffs differ from the simple rappel learned on practice climbs.

Rappel Points. It is of the utmost importance that the rappel point be absolutely sound, and the rope properly attached to it. Most rappel fatalities have occurred when the rappel sling broke or came off the point. Stout trees or bushes make excellent rappel points, and really sound chockstones, protruding blocks, and flakes are good. Several safe rappel points are shown in Figure 3-2. When a

suitable natural feature is lacking, a dependable piton can
be used, sometimes two or three pitons spaced to divide the
strain. If you cannot find a safe rappel point, you must climb
down until you come to one.

The rappel must be rigged so the rope can be retrieved by
pulling one end from below. Jamming or excessive friction
usually occurs if the rope is placed directly around the rappel
point (an exception might be a tree trunk). The connecting
link between point and rope is usually a strong sling, long
enough to hang free. It may have to be strung through the
piton eyes, or tied around a chockstone; use a carefully tied
water knot, and overhand safety knots, to retie the ends to
form the loop. Sometimes the sling can just be dropped over
the chosen point or flake; make very sure it will stay there.
If it is long enough, it may be placed double behind the point
chosen, and one side of the loop threaded through the opposite side to hang free in front. If the sling has to go over sharp
edges, pad it with paper, rags, or whatever you have. *Never*
trust an old sling found in place on the rock; it may be weak
from age, or from the friction engendered by the previous
rappel rope being pulled down. Don't even trust your own
slings too far; two are often rigged for double protection.
Only in real desperation does the average climber use carabiners for setting rappels, since they cannot be regained.

Rappel Rope. The rappel is usually made on the doubled
climbing rope. If two ropes are available, they are tied together. If there is only one climbing rope and longer rappels
are planned, a quarter-inch nylon auxiliary rope can be
carried.

The two halves of the rappel rope are coiled separately,
and one of the coils is passed through the loop of the sling.

To save wear on the middle of the rope, have slightly different portions of the rappel rope bear on the slings at different times. Each half of the coiled rappel rope is thrown outward down the cliff—one half at a time. While throwing, be sure that someone holds onto the rope so it won't escape. Several tries may be needed to get the ends well down, especially with a light line. Some climbers throw down each half in two parts: first the upper part and then the end part. If the rope ends will not go down well, the first man rappelling has to untangle them en route, of course using only his upper hand unless he finds a ledge to stand on.

Sling Rappels. On long or steep rappels, many climbers modify the body rappel position to reduce friction. One popular technique is the sling rappel. A trustworthy sling about five feet in circumference is twisted once, into a figure eight, with the knot to one side. Place each foot in one-half of the figure eight, and pull the sling up to your crotch. It should be the right size so you can hold the two sides where they cross, and pull them up in front a few inches above your crotch. Still holding these two portions of the sling in front of you, put three carabiners over them side by side (safer, and easier on the rope, than one). Pass the doubled rappel rope through the three carabiners, and turn the middle carabiner so the three gates face in alternating directions. From the carabiners (instead of from one hip as in the body rappel) the rope goes over one shoulder and is grasped below in the opposite hand, as illustrated in Figure 3-2. Rappelling then proceeds exactly as in the body rappel. Additional padding may be required at the shoulder. A sling rappel cannot be used when two ropes are tied together unless the knot is near

THREE SOUND RAPPEL POINTS

SLING RAPPEL

Figure 3-2

the rappel point, as knots will not go through the carabiners (it is a shock to discover this in mid-air).

Starting the Rappel. Be absolutely sure that you are in the rope correctly. This is sometimes confusing when you start the rappel from an awkward or precarious position, but it *must* be right. If you have to get into the rope above the rappel point, you must climb down below the point before actually starting to rope down.

Descending. The most experienced climber usually goes first, to straighten the ropes and select the next rappel point. Descending a known route is desirable, as it assures the rope reaching from one rappel point to the next, not always visible from above. (On the rare occasion when no stopping place can be found and the man cannot climb the rock, prusiking can be employed to re-ascend.) While the first man rappels, the others should closely watch the rappel point and sling, so they can give warning or take action if any sign of weakness occurs. When off rappel, the first man down tests the rope to make sure it can be retrieved; if it jams, the climbers above must re-arrange it. The second most experienced should come down last. To make sure the two portions of rope are not twisted around each other, he should keep a finger of the upper hand between them. A glove protects the finger but is not a requisite.

All should try not to strain the rappel point, or to dislodge rocks either with their feet or with the rope. The exact route of ascent is not necessarily the best rappel route; in fact, it is quite likely not to be. While rappelling, you tend to hang right below the rappel point, but can walk yourself readily to one side or the other to find smooth, sound portions of the cliff to descend. If you go over an overhang, give a little push or jump when your upper hand comes to the lip to prevent abrading your hand between rock and rope. When you first hang free, you may pendulum a bit to one or the other side, depending on the location of the rappel point. If a free rappel is very long, you dangle and turn gently in the air because you have no footing. Descend slowly so you don't get too hot. And most especially here, don't let go.

Pulling Down the Rope. When the entire party is down, untwist the two strands of rope if they have become twisted around each other. The rope is retrieved by hauling on the end that has the knot below the sling (keep track of this). If there is no knot, pull the end that comes easiest. A smooth, steady, and rather fast pull is the surest way to get the rope down. Two people can pull alternately to keep it moving. When the rope end starts to fall, duck! If the rope jams and will not come after you have pulled and jerked in every direction, someone has to climb up as far as necessary to free it, or as far as he can, with or without belay. Do not trust one end of a jammed rope for support, as it can come unstuck at any time. If you cannot climb high enough to free it, cut off what you can salvage, to help on the rest of the descent.

Choosing and Caring for Equipment

When you start climbing second, and leading, you need and want more equipment of your own. You have studied and used various kinds of ropes, slings, and hardware, appropriate to your local type of climbing; and undoubtedly have listened to endless discussions as to the merits of each. Thus you can make a choice without depending on possibly faulty sales advice, or being unduly tempted by unneeded and poorly understood gadgets. The major items which you will probably gradually add to your gear are discussed, with attention also to care, inspection, and periodic replacement.

Climbing Rope

A good, standard American climbing rope, chosen by many climbers of average ability for all-around use, is a 7/16-inch Goldline, 120 feet long. This rope weighs about six and a half pounds. It is made of hard-lay nylon. Three-eighths-inch Goldline is used when light weight is of importance and long falls are improbable.

Ropes used by some expert rock climbers may be longer or of different diameters, either because of personal preferences or for special uses. Some climbers like the imported Perlon ropes of the so-called kernmantel construction (a fiber core covered with a colored woven sheath). Kernmantel ropes are sometimes coiled in the hand, rather than around the foot.

The rope is the most expensive single piece of equipment, and with proper care and good luck should last for several years. Before each climb, inspect it very carefully for signs of excessive wear or damage, as evidenced by distinct changes in texture. Every bit of the rope is run through the hands and examined. Be especially thorough in inspecting club ropes, as you are unfamiliar with their previous use. Consult an experienced acquaintance if in doubt as to the rope's safety. A worn rope, or one which has held a very severe fall, should be replaced.

A pre-cut rope probably has the ends treated before purchase. If you buy a length from a large coil, see that the ends are taped before you take it, and give them additional care before using the rope. Remove the temporary taping and melt the ends over a flame, shaping them so the diameter will not exceed that of the rope. Tape the ends with several tight turns of vinyl tape. Whipping the ends with tough, fine cord is more elegant and permanent—also more trouble. The center of the climbing rope should also be marked with vinyl tape. All ropes get to looking much like others. The ends can be bound or otherwise distinguished in such a manner or color that you (and others) can tell to whom the rope belongs. Do not mark the center of the rope with lacquer or paint, as some chemicals weaken nylon, but the few inches at each end can be treated imaginatively.

A rope which has long been in a coil has to have the kinks removed. It can be dragged full length over a clean surface, or let down over a cliff or out of a high window to unwind. The process may need occasional repetition, especially when the rope is new or has been wet. Your rope should be stored in a coil, away from direct sunlight, sharp objects, excessive heat and chemicals. It should be stored dry; if it is wet, uncoil it, let it dry, and re-coil it. Never use your climbing rope for any but its intended purpose. If it has to be moved en masse on a climb, don't drag it in the dirt; pick it up in a bunch, or do it up in some type of quick-carry coil. Nobody must step on it. And try to keep it out of the way of rockfall, as a nylon rope cuts easily.

Pitons

As illustrated in Figure 2-9, they vary from huge bongs to tiny rurps ("Realization of Ultimate Reality Pitons"), with many types of wafers, blades, angles, and other styles. They are made of various alloys; many are of very strong chrome-molybdenum steel. Pitons are often manufactured and given special names by well-known climbers in both Europe and America. Sizes, shapes, and number needed depend on local rock conditions and the climber himself. You can identify your own by marking them with a distinctive color of paint— or, more permanently, by hammering in your initial with a steel die purchased at a hardware store.

If it is necessary to straighten bent pitons while on a climb, they can be flattened reasonably well by being hammered against a rock. However, pitons bent cold often crack. Straightened pitons must be inspected very carefully for signs of stress in the metal. The primary point of weakness is where the head joins the shaft, especially in horizontal pitons. It is preferable to wait until an anvil is available. Badly deformed pitons should be heated to an orange color, if facilities are available, before straightening. The piton may be permanently a bit weaker, due to the heat, but is less apt to crack in the straightening process. When the tips of pitons become wavy and uneven, they should be pounded flat. Any sharp corners should be filed or ground to a rounded edge.

Bolts

A protective device used where protection or aid is necessary, and there are no piton cracks. Bolts are used occasionally by average climbers; and frequently by climbers doing advanced specialized types of rock climbing on smooth faces. The basic principle is to drill a hole in the rock; drive in a stud which stays in by an expansion or a contraction principle; and fasten on an exterior hanger, which takes the place of the piton eye. Bolt kits, and assorted bolt hardware, are sold in mountaineering shops. Obviously the techniques should be practiced before they are used in serious climbing.

Nuts

A fairly new protective device (unrelated to bolts) developed in England. The "nuts" now in climbing use are manufactured for the purpose, in various sizes and shapes, usually of aluminum alloy. They have a hole or holes threaded with slings or wire cable. The idea is to drop them into cracks that flare out behind the opening. Sometimes a light hammer tap is necessary to set them soundly. Clip the carabiner through the sling. Test by jerking the sling hard at every possible angle of pull. After use, the nuts are removed with an upward jerk (aided by taps with the hammer if necessary).

Carabiners

Good ones are not among the cheapest, and are sold under their manufacturers' names. They should be chosen for strength, light weight, and smooth operation of the gate. Keep them out of dust and grit because of the gate mechanism. Never oil carabiners, as dirt sticks to oil.

Slings

Materials for slings, and many of their uses, have already been dwelt upon. Other uses include using a sling for protection instead of a piton. A really strong one can, for instance, be looped around a rock point, pulled under a chock-stone, or doubled around a bush, and attached with a cara-biner to the climbing rope.

Instead of tying directly to the climbing rope, some climbers wear a fifteen- to thirty-foot length of one-inch nylon web-bing wound around the waist. This is called a Swami belt, and is much more comfortable than the rope in case of a fall. After winding most of the webbing around the waist, secure it with a water knot. Attach the climbing rope to the coil of webbing with a double-knotted bowline, which is tied exactly like an ordinary bowline except for making two loops (one on top of the other) instead of one, and inserting the end of the rope through both at once.

Helmets and Hats

Due to the disproportionate number of head injuries in climbing (from both falling rock and injuries sustained in falls), hard hats or helmets are now commonly seen on rock climbers. They are sold in mountaineering shops. Necessary features include a good fit; a dependable and adjustable chin strap; and particularly the manufacturer's name, the date of manufacture, and the certification mark of the Snell Memorial Foundation to assure a specified performance in actual tests. Helmets weigh between one and one and a half pounds, and come in many colors.

A plain felt hat is preferable to climbing bareheaded. It cushions the head from minor blows, protects from sunburn, shades glasses in the rain, and keeps dirt and sun out of the eyes. A felt hat (removed from the head) is also useful as insulation against a rope burn in rappelling.

Clothing

It is often far hotter or colder on the rocks than on the ground; season, climate, storm, and whether the climb will be in sun or shade, should be allowed for. *Kletterschuhe*, if tight enough for rock climbing, are miserable for hiking; take extra boots and socks on long approaches. Comfort and safety are of value, but fashion too has a place. Corduroy knickers are the New Look on the rocks. But, alas, rocks are so abrasive that climbers, at least in the United States, are the world's worst-dressed sportsmen.

Miscellaneous

Carry a pocketknife. Supply sunglasses if needed. If you wear prescription glasses, make sure they cannot fall off.

Rock Climbing Places and Precautions

Naturally rock climbing is most popular in areas where the rock is beautifully adapted to the sport—Yosemite-type granite, for instance. In popular areas, routes are so well established that they all have names, usually descriptive, alarming, whimsical, or humorous in nature. As an intermediate climber who is beginning to fend for himself and take responsibility for others, you will, if possible, gravitate to such places. Otherwise you will make do with what you have. Perhaps a rock is a rock is a rock. Certainly you are hooked when you begin to trace out routes on every rock you see.

In non-mountainous areas, there are bluffs, palisades,

cliffs, ravines, quarries, boulders, and even road cuts where you can sharpen your techniques. With or without good climbing nearby, you may yearn to travel to other areas, usually places you have heard about, read about, or seen pictured. With modified techniques and equipment to suit the place, every area has its own appeal.

Extra care is required on unfamiliar or unclimbed routes, when you are a long ways from help, and when the weather is adverse. The climber functions less efficiently in extremes of heat, wind, and cold. Sudden changes in weather can transform conditions from good to bad instantaneously. Wet or snowy rocks are infinitely more difficult and dangerous than dry ones. Weather may force a retreat. Other reasons for turning back despite the strong urge to finish a climb include incompetence, fright, unwillingness or illness in the party, unexpected route difficulties; and an "off day" for the leader.

Probably the most common reason for giving up a climb is lack of time to finish it before dark. In deciding whether to go on or retreat, remember that it may be quicker to finish the climb if the top is nearer than the bottom, if the climbing ahead is known to be easier than that behind, *and* if there is a way to walk down.

Roped climbing and rappelling in the dark are very dangerous. If night overtakes you on the cliffs, tie on well in as good a spot as you can find, and stay put till daylight. And when setting out next morning, compensate for the long hard night by using extra care.

When you become adept at all this, you will no longer be

a beginner, or even an advanced beginner. You may be well on the way to becoming a specialist and an expert in rock climbing. And sooner or later you may begin to think of rock climbing as only one branch of the complex sport of mountaineering, which has other types of terrain to offer.

chapter four

Equipment and Techniques
For Snow Climbing

AS is readily deduced from inspecting mountains with the idea of climbing them, some routes are all rock, others all snow and ice, and many are a combination. A safe ascent of a route involving snow and ice requires a familiarity with, and a respect for, the substance. You must also have the proper equipment and know how to use it.

Danger of Snow and Ice Slopes

People who would never think of climbing a cliff, or who have some understanding of rock but none of snow, seem to be easily fooled by the hidden hazards of snow and ice. Those who live in areas with cold winters know it is easy to slip on level ice but may have no conception of how much easier, farther, and harder they can fall when it is steep. Those who live in mild climates near sea level have provided a startling record of disasters on icy mountain slopes. Imbued with enthusiasm and ignorance, they rush out on snowy hillsides which are as pretty as Christmas cards—only to shoot off like toboggans to injury or death. Others, lightly dressed, set forth across snows that look innocent and beautiful on a springlike day, but lose their lives in sudden storms.

Safe Climbing on Snow and Ice

An elementary knowledge of proper equipment, clothing, and techniques would avert many such accidents, both among non-climbers and would-be climbers. If you are well versed in basic rock climbing techniques, you have a head start, though there is no reason other than geographical chance or personal preference for taking up one phase of climbing before the other. In fact, the two can be learned simultaneously, and some of the techniques are very similar. As in rock climbing, snow and ice techniques are best learned through instruction and practice with able and experienced individuals or groups, or in qualified courses or schools. Reading is helpful, but is no substitute for workouts under skilled instructors. Beginners should start their practice on snow, or on snow that has a frozen icy surface; this is the limited meaning of "snow and ice" as used in this chapter.

Equipment for Snow and Ice Climbing

To start rock climbing, you can turn up in some old clothes and climb, but for snow, you *must* have the proper clothing and gear. If you wish to try equipment out before buying, it can be rented from a mountaineering shop, borrowed from a friend, or provided by a commercial climbing school or guide service. However it is acquired, its selection and care is similar.

Ice Axe

A special-purpose tool exquisitely designed for safeguarding and assisting the traveler on steep snow and ice. Most are imported from Europe and Japan. The axe, as illustrated in Figure 4-1, has a wooden shaft, oval in cross section, about twenty-six to forty inches long. At one end of the shaft is a steel point or spike; at the other end is a head between ten and twelve inches long. It consists of a sharp pick, and a blade or adze which is either flat or slightly curved. Most axes have a wrist loop made of three-quarter-inch webbing or leather attached to the shaft by a glide ring. A metal stop, nine or ten inches from the tip, keeps the glide ring from falling off.

Despite differences in style, details, and prices, any standard ice axe gives good service. Do not buy one with a small, substandard head. Choose an axe of sturdy workman-like construction, and pay particular heed to the shaft. Though hickory is regarded by Americans as tops for tool handles, Europeans use ash (having no native hickory trees). A straight close grain, free of knots, should be chosen. As to length, select an axe that feels comfortable in the hand as a staff. Too long a handle is awkward on steep slopes and is a nuisance to carry; some excellent climbers recommend a very short axe regardless of the person's height.

The shaft is sometimes wrapped, for three or four inches above the point, with vinyl tape to save the wood from excessive abrasion. Occasional sanding and a light rubbing with hot boiled linseed oil will protect the handle from water. If the shaft breaks, it can be replaced. The wrist loop should be checked occasionally for wear, and replaced if necessary. Store the axe in a dry place. Your living quarters are ideal—and quite practical, as an ice axe is not only useful but decorative.

Boots

Important to protect the feet and give proper traction on snow. The best boot is a European (or European type) mountaineering boot, six or sometimes eight inches high, padded under the lining with foam rubber. The sole has rubber lugs, whose great utility lies in their adaptability to snow and wet or dry rock. Nylon or waxed cotton boot laces are best.

The boots should be large enough to be worn over at least two pairs of heavy wool socks, and still leave room to wiggle your toes. They should have hard box toes to protect the feet when kicking steps and when crampons are strapped to the boots. Waterproof construction is essential; look for a water welt, a very narrow strip of leather sewn to the uppers and the sole. The tongue should be sewn shut at least partway up, and many are sewn clear to the top.

Your boots must be cared for to maintain their waterproof properties and protect the leather. After use, let them dry slowly; stuff tightly with newspaper, which should be changed occasionally, or use a boot tree while they are drying, to maintain their shape. Treat the leather with a thin liquid silicone; apply a second coat to seams and edges of the sole. Then rub in a coat of *wax*-based waterproofing (not grease or oil). Warm the boots before or after the application in the sun, next to a hot air register, or in an oven which has been heated to about 140 degrees and turned off before putting the boots in (setting them on aluminum foil protects the soles from the hot grill). Keep your boots in good repair, and store them clean and waxed in an airy place.

Crampons

Not usually essential for the strict neophyte, but a fundamental piece of snow and ice gear. As illustrated in Figure 4-1, they are assemblages of sharp metal spikes on a (usually) hinged framework which, when strapped tightly to the boots, provide stability on hard snow and ice. They come with ten or twelve points each (four-point instep crampons are not real climbing irons). Ten-point crampons are satisfactory for all-round use on easy to moderate climbs. Crampons with twelve points, two sticking out in front to kick into steep ice, are essential for advanced ice work. Good crampons are made from tempered steel, by forging. Army-surplus crampons are cheap but untrustworthy.

Boots and crampons must work as a solid unit; hence a good fit is essential. First choose your boots, and have them with you when you are buying or renting crampons. It should require some force to jam the boot into the crampon. The boot must not slip sideways; the crampon must be long enough that the front points are near the boot toe, but short enough so the front ring or hook of the harnessing framework is well back of the front end of the boot. A pair of crampons has a right and left, important for a perfect fit. Some crampons are adjustable for different sizes of boots.

The crampon is held on partly by the tight fit and a piece

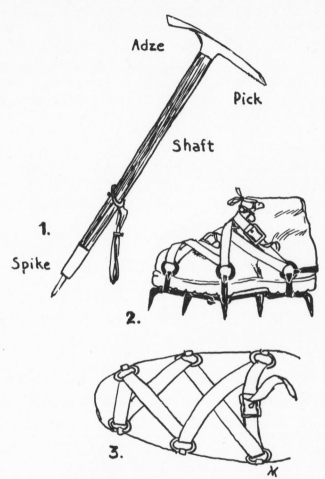

1. Adze

Pick

Shaft

Spike

2.

3.

1: ICE AXE.   2: BOOT AND CRAMPON.
3: SINGLE-STRAP CRAMPON LACING.

Figure 4-1

of metal that fits around the heel of the boot; and partly by a series of straps and buckles, or by a single strap five or six feet long. This may be a thong of leather or a strap of cotton or linen webbing three-quarters-inch wide. It must be long enough so there is an ample end to pull on when cinching it up tight over boots, socks, pant legs, and gaiters. Excess strap can be tucked in. Understand the method of attachment when you get your crampons. The standard method of lacing the long single strap is shown in Figure 4-1. Minor adjustments for fit are possible, but must be made with great care lest the metal be weakened or broken. Keep crampons free of rust. File the points sharp again if they become dulled. Check the straps occasionally, and replace if signs of wear appear.

Rope

Essential in ice work, but the beginner is not expected to supply it while learning. Exclusively for snow and ice work, a 60-foot, 3/8-inch Goldline would be adequate for two people. However, anyone expecting to do much climbing should have an all-purpose rope at least 120 feet long, and 7/16 inches in diameter, that can be used for two people on both rock and snow and for three people primarily on snow and glaciers.

A rope that has become thoroughly soaked or even superficially wet should receive special attention at the end of the climbing day. It should be uncoiled, and dried under natural conditions (not by the campfire!). Kinks should be removed, both before and after drying. It should be re-coiled for storage.

Ice Pitons and Screws

Employed primarily by advanced climbers, for protection on difficult ice climbs. Intermediate climbers may want a few along for practice, for protection on an unexpectedly steep or icy slope, or for emergencies in which an anchor is necessary and possible. Keep in mind that ice pitons will usually hold only a fraction of the strain that a rock piton can withstand. Superior protection is obtained where it is possible to drive rock pitons into sound rock walls.

Ice pitons are generally between six and twelve inches long and have large eyes. Some resemble large rock pitons. Some are tubular, with or without threads; and some are made like very long, rather thin screws. A hammer, or a short axe with a hammer head instead of an adze, is needed to drive the unthreaded pitons and to start the screws. The screws can be turned, after starting, with another piton or the axe point inserted in the eye for leverage. If possible, ice pitons and screws should be placed at an angle slightly uphill from the perpendicular to the line of potential pull. Snow pickets, aluminum tubes about four feet long, are sometimes carried for use as pitons by parties expecting quite difficult snow passages.

Clothing for Snow and Ice Conditions

Adequate clothing must be available for protection against cold, damp, sudden storm, temperature extremes, and exposure to sun.

Underwear

Wool, or part-wool and part-cotton, is the best material.

Dacron, down, and the like insulate well while dry; cotton "fishnet" underwear is intended for use under such materials to allow perspiration to escape. But only wool continues to feel warm against the skin even when it has gotten wet (from inside or outside). Underwear with long legs is essential unless the outer pants are of wool, and is sometimes needed even then. Separate uppers and lowers are more adjustable to changing temperatures than one-piece outfits.

Pants

These should be of a hard-weave material that does not collect snow. Wool, part-wool, and nylon are good. Heavy cotton is all right if it is water-repellent (denim is unacceptable). Be sure your pants are baggy enough for freedom of movement. Knickers, often corduroy, are popular, especially in the summer (although corduroy gets wet easily and dries slowly). Trousers should taper toward the feet, and should be held down by an elastic under the instep or tied around the ankle with a drawstring.

Socks

All-wool is the only suitable material, except for a little nylon reinforcing. It is usual to wear at least two heavy pairs, with a light soft pair (which may be nylon or fine wool) next to the foot to reduce friction if blisters are a serious problem. With knickers, wear one pair of long socks that reach to the knees or above them. Spare dry socks must be carried on long climbs, as wet socks promote frostbite.

Gaiters

Essential to keep snow out of boot tops. A compact, efficient type is four to eight inches high, tubular with elastic at top and bottom. For deep snow, they should extend up to just below the knee. Short gaiters are of nylon or water-repellent cotton, with or without a side zipper. Long ones, of heavy-duty material, usually have hook lacings. Instep cords or straps hold the gaiters down; to prevent cutting these straps, do not fasten them until you are on snow. Gaiters are also useful to keep gravel out of boot tops.

Shirts and Sweaters

Several lightweight layers (instead of one heavy one) permit you to add or subtract garments as temperature vascillations require. Since a snow climb can be extremely hot, the bottom layer is often a cotton T-shirt or a long-sleeved cotton shirt that is cool but protects against sunburn. Other shirts and sweaters should be woolen.

Parka and Poncho

A generously cut, windproof, water-repellent parka is a necessity. It can be worn as a light jacket, or it goes over the woolen garments when wind, cold, or precipitation requires. It should have many pockets, and a hood is essential. Choose a sturdy cotton poplin or a cotton-nylon weave, with or without front zipper. You can rewaterproof your parka when necessary with a wax-emulsion solution or a spray-can compound; or have a dry cleaning establishment do it. A lightweight plastic poncho is useful in case of summer rains or sloppy snowfall too extensive for the parka to cope with. A *cagoule* is a sort of hybrid parka-raincoat, long enough to keep the pants dry but too long to climb in.

Down Clothing

Down jackets and trousers are very warm, very expensive, and not needed for the type of trips that the beginner goes on, although marvelous on expeditions and winter ascents, etc. Extra wool socks are far more versatile than down "bootees" for ordinary climbs.

Hat, Cap, Mittens

Helmets and hard hats are coming into use in snow and ice work; they provide protection against head injuries suffered from falling rocks or from crashing into rocks. For beginning practice trips, it is sufficient to wear a felt hat with a brim for sun protection. A woolen cap should be available, as much warmth is lost through the head. A pair of woolen mittens (warmer than finger gloves) should be carried. An extra pair, and/or a pair of nylon or water-repellent canvas "covers" should be taken on all trips longer than a few hours.

Sun Protection

Sunburn is an acute problem on snow because of reflection, especially at high elevations. Goggles or dark glasses are essential. A good sunburn cream (the popular beach types are inadequate) can be had from mountaineering shops or pharmacies. Special preparations are manufactured for the lips, which are especially sun-sensitive. Clown white (actors' grease paint) or zinc oxide ointment give almost complete protection for people who sunburn severely. Remember to apply the goo to areas affected by reflection, and to *re*-apply as often as needed, especially around nose and mouth.

Where to Learn

As a neophyte suitably clothed and outfitted, you are far better off than an unequipped visitor to the snow slopes. You must, however, practice the proper handling and use of your equipment under able tutelage. The group or individual giving instruction should select a safe practice slope, its steepness correlated with the texture of the snow. It must have a safe runout, without rocks, trees, or precipices at the bottom. This easy slope will ideally allow you to practice all the techniques basic to safe snow and ice climbing.

Ice Axe Techniques

Aside from proper boots, the ice axe is the *sine qua non* of snow and ice climbing. It is in constant use whether or not rope and crampons are needed. The major functions of the axe's parts are these: (1) Point or spike: used like the bottom end of a cane in walking, or to drive into the snow for stability when climbing. (2) Adze or blade: for cutting steps in hard snow. (3) Pick: for cutting steps in ice, for self-arrests when falling, or to jam into steep snow so the axe handle can be used for balance. (4) Shaft: to use as a staff, and as a belay point for the rope.

The many uses of the ice axe are mastered with practice, and during this practice its three sharp parts must be recognized as dangerous and be treated with care and respect.

Transporting and Carrying the Ice Axe

While not in use, the axe is often equipped with a rubber guard over the point, and sometimes an adjustable sheath for the head. To carry the axe when walking, hold the shaft at the balance point. Carry it parallel with the ground, point forward and head backward with the pick pointing down. It may also be tucked under one arm in this position. When the axe is used as a walking stick, the head provides comfortable support for the hand, with the pick facing forward.

Wrist Loop

Used only in places where the axe is essential to safety, yet would be lost if dropped. The clasp slides to tighten the loop after the hand is inserted. Some excellent climbers are against wrist loops, claiming the axe might injure you if attached to the wrist, and should never be dropped anyway. These considerations, while valid, seem to be outweighed by the importance of having your axe when it is needed.

Walking up Easy Slopes

Walking up the practice slope is no problem, but it is the beginning of learning to climb on steep snow. Start straight up the slope, kicking your toes into the snow. Footsteps should be fairly close together to conserve energy and accommodate those with short legs who may be coming after you. Use the axe as a staff, with the pick backward. With the hand in this position on the head, the axe is ready for instantaneous use if a self-arrest is required. When the angle steepens, start to make switchbacks. Hold the axe in the uphill hand; change it to the other hand when you change direction. On a slippery slope, stop moving and change the axe to the other hand before turning. Plant each foot firmly so the lugs bite into the snow; stamp or kick footsteps if the snow surface requires. Develop a gait in which you tend to drop your weight over the forward foot at each step. Keep your weight directly above your feet for balance; if you lean into the slope, your feet tend to skid out from under you. When several people ascend together, each should walk some little distance behind the other, all using the same footsteps and improving on them (it takes far less energy than for each to make his own steps).

Self-Arrests

An important function of the ice axe is to slow or stop your own slide after a fall. It is a vital skill, whether you are roped or unroped. It is learned on safe slopes and soft snow. Protect yourself from sharp ice particles with long sleeves and mittens. Hold the axe in the arrest position, as follows: Hold the axe head near your shoulder, with fingers over the head and thumb under the adze. The pick points forward so it will dig into the snow when you fall on the axe. The shaft is held diagonally across your chest with the other hand grasping it near the tip. The tip is held near your hip.

Next, lie facedown in the snow, with the axe under you, as shown in Figure 4-2. Let yourself slide downhill feet first; arch your back slightly to press the pick into the snow under your shoulder. The friction of pick in snow should gradually stop your fall. Repeat on increasingly steep or fast slopes.

On fast crusty snow, start the pressure at once, but drive the pick in gradually and take care not to let the point catch and flip you over. As the slide becomes faster, spread your legs for balance. In soft snow, dig in your knees and toes (and elbows too) to assist in the arrest; in hard snow brake with the toes of your boots in addition to the axe.

As a real fall is not always in a conveniently perfect arrest position, practice getting into that position from various awkward starts. Start sliding on back or side; curl your body a bit and roll over quickly toward the side on which you are holding the axe head. Start down head first, on your stomach; dig in the pick; and to get your legs downhill, swing them around the pivot formed by the pick. Start down on your back, head downhill; roll onto your stomach and then pivot into the feet-first position. And act quickly, before you get going too fast.

When you start climbing potentially dangerous slopes, always note the consequences of a slip. Observe the gradient and texture of the snow, and the length and nature of the runout. Mentally rehearse the motions for a quick self-arrest.

Rope Techniques for Snow and Ice Climbing

If self-arrests always worked, there would be no need of a rope. However, on slopes very soft, very hard, comparatively steep, or with dangerous runouts, the climber cannot always stop himself soon enough, if at all. Hence, as on steep rocks, the roped team is used for mutual protection.

Roping Up

The preferred number of climbers on one rope for snow

THE SELF-ARREST

Figure 4-2

and ice is three. A shorter rope is used than in most rock climbing; 120 feet for three people is standard. If the available rope is longer, or if only two are tying into a 120-foot rope, it can be shortened. One climber ties to the end of the rope with the usual bowline, but leaves about two feet extra at the end. The unwanted portion of rope is wound diagonally around the chest, over one shoulder and under the opposite arm. The coil is then secured with a bowline-on-a-coil tied with the rope end saved for that purpose (see Fig. 2-3). The middle man should not use the butterfly knot in snow work, as it jams when wet. The easiest substitute is the double bowline, tied like a standard bowline but using a doubled section in the middle of the rope, as illustrated in Figure 2-1.

Methods of Climbing

As in rock climbing, the best climber goes first, and the least experienced last. There are two methods of progress, continuous and consecutive (both also employed on rocks of ease or difficulty).

Continuous Climbing. Used where a fall can be stopped even though the climbers are in motion. The rope is needed for protection because of crevasses on a glacier, and/or steepness. All those tied together walk at the same time, each adjusting his pace to the others. They are far enough apart so there is little or no slack in the rope between them, except that each climber holds one or two coils of rope in his free hand, to help adjust his pace to the others and to allow a slight warning in case of a fall. Each climber should have an ice axe (a beginner will feel he has too many things in his hands). When one climber changes direction at the corners of the switchbacks, and has to change the axe and coil to opposite hands, the others should wait until the transfer is complete.

Consecutive Climbing. Used when the ascent is steeper, the snow icier, or the terrain below dangerous—and where it would be hard to hold a fall without being set for it. Only one climber moves at a time while the other two belay him. The sequence of climbing is much like that of multi-pitch rock climbing. The leader goes up a rope length; he brings up the second and climbs another rope length; and the second brings up the third before joining the leader.

Rope Handling

In handling the rope on snow and ice climbing, due allowance has to be made for moisture and temperature. In cold, dry weather on hard snow, the rope may stay dry even if dragged all over the snow. If the snow is deep or wet, the rope is almost sure to get wet sooner or later. You can put this off a little by trying to keep it out of the snow when climbing continuously, perhaps hanging your coil on the axe head instead of laying it in the snow, etc. The wetter the rope, the harder it is to handle because of weight and friction. More moisture is transferred to clothing, especially mittens. Knots are harder to tie and untie in a wet rope. When the temperature drops, the rope freezes and gets slippery, stiff, perhaps covered with hoarfrost. When it does get wet and frozen, endure it.

Belaying on Snow and Ice

Establishing a solid belay is more difficult on snow than on rock because of the slippery and unbroken nature of the climbing medium. A hip belay, as in rock work, can be given if the belayer is well braced in depressions, holes, small crevasses, flat places, or on various stances manufactured with the axe. However, the usual stopping place consists of two footsteps. The ice axe jammed into the snow is then used (something like an anchor piton and carabiner) as a fixed object around which the rope is passed. A simple belay around the axe shaft may serve when the axe is especially stable. Much stronger is the boot-axe belay.

Boot-Axe Belay

The ice axe and the boot work together to establish a belay point which is unlikely to be jerked out of the snow, and which provides much better friction for the rope than is possible with the axe shaft alone. The belay position is pictured in Figure 4-3. To give the boot-axe belay: (1) Stand sideways to the slope, facing in the general direction of the person climbing. (2) Kick or cut two sound and ample footsteps, one uphill and slightly in front of the other. (3) On the uphill side of the upper footstep, drive the axe as far as possible down into the snow, with the pick pointing uphill. (4) Plant the outside of the uphill boot firmly against the downhill side of the axe shaft. Place the downhill foot in its footstep. (5) The rope that comes from the climber should be passed over the toe of the boot; around the axe handle; then downhill between the axe handle and the instep; and back uphill toward the boot heel, as illustrated. The belay rope is held in the downhill hand. For holding a fall, friction is increased by moving the belay hand backwards and uphill

Figure 4-3

above the ankle (hence this boot-axe arrangement is called the S-bend, to distinguish it from other positions that give less friction). When the position is fully understood, you can apply it very rapidly by jamming the axe point into the snow in the proper relationship to the rope, and stamping your foot against the shaft almost simultaneously. (6) As the up-hill hand grasps the axe head, lean over the axe so your weight holds it down into the snow.

Belay Practice

Falls should be held for practice as in rock climbing. Start by belaying the climber who is coming up from below. You have to take your hand off the axe to pull in slack; but this hand is immediately returned to the axe head, with your weight over it, if a fall occurs. Increasingly severe falls should be tried. Belay the leader in the same position as when giving an upper belay. Remember that the shock will be greater. In choosing your stance consider the direction in which he will fall, and where he will hang when you catch the fall. The principle of the dynamic belay should be applied by letting the rope run a bit—you cannot help it if the jolt is severe—to lessen the shock on the axe.

Team Belays

In snow climbing, no one person on the rope is completely responsible for holding a fall. The person falling should immediately go into a self-arrest. Others on the rope should always belay, or be poised to belay, anyone who falls. Sometimes one climber has to catch two or more who are falling together. Whenever the cry "Fall!" is heard, others on the rope go instantly into a belay position if they are not already in it. The ascent of increasingly difficult slopes becomes relatively safe with known techniques of rope protection, belays, and uses of the ice axe.

Ascending Difficult Slopes

As steeper slopes are climbed, on snow that is icier, or deeper and softer and less stable, methods learned and practiced so far are applied with greater finesse. The axe is used not only as a staff but as a sort of handhold when needed. In soft, unstable snow, the shaft is sunk deeply on the uphill side at each step. In especially precarious places, it is moved from one hole to the next only while the climber is standing still. Where the snow is hard or icy, either point or pick may be used on the uphill side for balance or for a slight purchase. The axe is used also to feel and probe the snow for changes in texture. Where kicking footsteps becomes arduous or ineffective, the adze can be used to cut footsteps. Care to maintain perfect balance is compulsory. Crampons are still another specialized piece of equipment to lessen the effort and hazard of ascending steep snow and ice.

Crampon Techniques

Your first try at walking up a crusty snow slope on crampons is apt to be wildly successful! The points bite crisply into the glittering white surface and your footing seems secure beyond human possibility. But as with other climbing equipment, crampons must be properly used to get the greatest benefit from their beautiful design, and to avoid inherent hazards.

Storage and Transport

The points of crampons are dangerous, and must be treated as such to prevent injuring yourself and others. They also must be protected to keep them sharp. Cover the points when out of use, and be careful when wearing them. Store crampons in a box, at home or in the car. On the pack, use bought rubber crampon protectors, or lash the pair points-down to opposite sides of a board or a rectangle of styrofoam. Corks, or sections of rubber tubing, can be stuck on all the points instead.

Learning to Walk on Crampons

You should have a frozen surface with a fairly gentle gradient to practice on. To put on the crampons, sit down where you can lay them with points down on the snow, and install first one and then the other. Straighten out the harness, shove your boot into the framework, and lash them tightly to your feet. Adjustment of the straps is usually necessary after walking a short distance. Make sure they are tight enough not to slip, but loose enough across the instep not to cut off your circulation. Take each step with the crampons flat on the snow surface. This requires great flexibility in the ankles. Place the foot down firmly and precisely with each step, stamping slightly or letting your body weight fall forward over the foot if necessary to drive the points into the snow. When taking a step, raise each foot high enough to prevent your tripping on the points.

Cautions in Crampon Use

One of the hazards in cramponing is the possibility of

catching the points on the clothing of the opposite leg. You may tear your clothes or your hide, or trip yourself. To prevent this, wear pants that are not too full in the legs, wrap baggy pant legs with cord, or wear confining gaiters. Knickers and long socks lessen but do not eliminate this hazard. Also learn to walk with your legs slightly apart. Perfect your balance. If you do fall, remember that the points may puncture someone, maybe you. In making a self-arrest when wearing crampons, bend the knees somewhat to avoid catching a crampon point and being flipped. Never step on the rope with crampons. In soft snow, watch out for the balls of snow that may form between the points. Knock them loose with a tap of the axe, or a kick with the side of one foot against the opposite boot.

Cramponing on Increasingly Difficult Slopes

Crampons are often used for convenience on hard snow that is quite flat, but their greatest use is on steep, icy slopes. Once put on for a climb, they are often worn all day long, even on sections where the snow or slope becomes easy, to save the trouble of removal and re-installing, But it is customary to take them off for all but the shortest rock passages, to protect the points from dulling or damage. You will probably not encounter really long, steep, icy slopes in your early climbs. But it is a somewhat relative matter; what takes all your skill and nerve during your first summer may seem easy in a season or two. As the slopes you climb become steeper and icier, be especially attentive to balance. Both feet and body are positioned somewhat as in friction-climbing on rock. Stamp the crampons flat to the slope and coordinate the use of crampons and axe; also pay close attention to belays and possible self-arrests. When the slope seems too icy or too steep for you to trust the bite of your crampons, the rope leader (or you yourself) can provide an additional safeguard by chopping steps. Up till then, the leader may have saved time and effort by cutting steps only at belay spots. Enjoy your crampons, perfect your mastery of them, and learn to trust them on both the ascent and the descent.

Descending Snow and Ice Slopes

The descent of a given slope is usually made in much the same manner and with the same equipment and protection as the ascent if conditions remain the same, but with even greater care, since the descent is often more awkward, and sometimes snow conditions are worse.

Climbing Down

If a steep ascent required careful climbing, the descent probably will too, though snow may be better or worse. The party uses the same footsteps if possible. The leader goes last in a roped party. Snow that was soft on the ascent may have grown icy, or hard snow may have softened and be poorly consolidated. The first person down should if necessary improve the old steps, or cut or kick new ones.

Walking Down

If the snow is soft and the slope fairly easy, nothing more specialized is required than walking down. Even this should be done properly, to perfect techniques and save energy and time. When you are going straight down, let your weight come down on your heel at each step, to drive it into the snow; keep your foot bent toe up so the heel hits first. You are least apt to slip out of this type of step. If the slope seems rather steep or the snow poorly consolidated, take each downward step with deliberate care, using your axe at your side as a staff held in both hands. On such a slope, the party may be roped but walk all together. If the snow is more reliable in texture, let each heel slide for a couple of feet in the "plunge step." This increases the speed and ease of descent. Under ideal conditions, you can run down a slope safely with the plunge step, holding the axe in arrest position.

Glissading

Glissading is a speedy, restful, and wonderful way to go down, when texture and gradient are just right. It is also potentially dangerous if you misjudge the slope and conditions. Practice on short slopes with obviously safe runouts. Gradually work up to longer and faster slopes. But *always* look for a safe runout as a safety measure if you should lose control, for instance by hitting an unexpectedly icy spot. It just isn't healthy to end a glissade in a rock pile or by shooting over a cliff.

Glissades are made sitting or standing. The sitting position is safest and easiest. To get ready, remove your crampons and stow them safely; batten down your clothing and put on mittens; hold the axe in arrest position, with the wrist loop on. Sit down with knees straight and take off. The point of the axe can be used in the snow at either side for a rudder to aid in slight changes of direction, or to slow you down a bit. If you want to stop, dig in your heels and your axe point, or roll over in a self-arrest. A major change in direction, to avoid obstacles below, must be accomplished by stopping, and traversing on foot to a new starting point. On quite soft snow, pillows of it may form under your behind; hunch over them. Rough terrain or small rocks may be rather bruising. The most uncomfortable effect is getting your clothes wet. If keeping dry is important, walk or make a standing glissade.

A standing glissade is done with more style and aplomb, and is suited to steeper slopes when sufficient experience and judgment have been gained. It is more strenuous on the legs too. It resembles skiing on the feet, with the axe (loop on wrist) used to one side for support and steering. The standing glissade must be undertaken by the beginning climber with great caution, and first used only on short slopes to get the feel of it. Good judgment of snow conditions in relation to the gradient, as well as skill at keeping the glissade under control, is required for all glissading that is done safely. And never fail to consider the runout.

Use your equipment until it no longer feels awkward; work on basic techniques until they become automatic both on practice slopes and on easy climbs. You are then ready to concentrate on the multitude of other factors which contribute to proficiency and judgment in ascents and descents on snow, ice, and glacier climbs.

chapter five

Snow, Ice, and Glacier Terrain

BESIDES technical skills, a growing knowledge of the complex environment encountered on snow and ice climbs is a necessary ingredient of safe mountain ascents. Such knowledge is gained bit by bit, over a period of many seasons, in many weathers, on diverse peaks. A theoretical acquaintance with the common conditions that you will encounter or should avoid will help you recognize and cope with them.

Where to Find Snow and Ice Climbing

The most obvious snow and ice climbing is on glacier peaks. However, it may be unrelated to the glaciers on a particular peak, or may exist on non-glacier peaks, where it is often found alternating with rock. Superficially, the same techniques are used on glacier or non-glacier snow work; actually, non-glacier snow work is much simpler. Excluding winter

103

ascents, which are not for the inexperienced, such terrain is encountered either early in the season, before most of the snow has melted; or on the north sides of peaks, in shaded couloirs, and on other parts of mountains where snow has piled deep and has been protected from the sun. Such areas often provide snow and ice routes during the summer, long after the opportunities of early-season climbing have melted away, especially in years of heavy or late snowfall.

Snow and Ice Conditions and Hazards

Routes involving snow and ice may be sought out for several reasons. You may want to gain experience on snow and ice even though you must climb in ranges which have few or no glaciers. Perhaps you cannot avoid it, prefer it, or find it easier than the rock. There are many obvious differences from rock climbing, and some less apparent.

Changes in Surface

Snow and ice are extremely variable. The surface changes with temperatures, elevation, exposure, weather and season. It changes from year to year, from day to day, and even from hour to hour. For instance, a particular couloir in the early spring thaws may be an unthinkable avalanche of water, sloppy snow, and rock coming down from the walls above. Similar conditions may exist after an unseasonable storm. In early summer the same gully may present an excellently consolidated surface. Or on hot days the snow may be crumbly and unstable. On a cold morning it may be so hard that crampons are needed, but by afternoon glissading may be possible.

A snow surface may change to ice at any step. There may be water-ice at the head of the couloir. By autumn, the gully may be almost dry or have melted down to old snow nearly as hard as ice. A new snowfall may mask conditions that exist just below the surface. Observation, calculation, and investigation will frequently be required before you decide on the route; sometimes you must choose a different route or give up the climb.

Similar changes in texture are constantly occurring on snowfields and slopes. A firm surface of consolidated summer snow is ideal to walk on—far easier than talus if there is a choice. If the snow is very hard or icy, you will need crampons. Snow that has alternately thawed and melted over a long period of time forms surface pits known as sun cups, separated by ridges. The sun cups often provide belay spots, and safe walking even on quite steep slopes. The pits become more pronounced as the season advances, and at times become so deep, with such high ridges between, that much energy is expended climbing from one to another.

A phenomenon that is of no importance in climbing, but is interesting since it is seldom seen by anyone but climbers, is red snow. This is the so-called "watermelon snow," named from the color and odor that suddenly bloom in each footstep or give a reddish cast to an entire snowfield. This effect is caused by certain algae (the most common is *Chlamydomonas nivalis*) which live in the snow, and develop red pigment during their resting stage in late summer.

Soft, wet, poorly consolidated snow, usually found between early- and mid-season climbing, may hold your weight at one step, yet allow your foot to plunge in deeply at the next. At best this is exhausting, and at worst unspeakable!

Your leg may become so heavily encased in snow that it will not come out of its hole, and has to be chopped free with your axe. Snow may also conceal the existence of lakes or streams under the surface. You can hear running streams, but there is no such warning of lakes in flat areas. You may suddenly find a foot many feet below the surface immersed in water. Try to get away from the lake or from the soft snow by changing course.

A similar situation arises when unbroken snow conceals rocks and talus which lie close to the surface with spaces melted around them. This is especially likely close to other rocks which protrude from the surface, and in the area where snow and talus meet. There is no sure way to avoid sinking down among the rocks when changing from talus to snow and vice versa, but the realization that this is apt to occur can prevent injury.

Melt Holes and Moats

Another condition due to melt is the deep holes that form around rocks and the moats along the bases of cliffs. In these places, the snow either did not pack well in the first place, or melted faster than the rest of the snow because the darker object beside it absorbed more heat. The same effect, though of minor importance in climbing, is observed where rocks have fallen to the snow surface and have melted deep holes due to absorption rather than reflection of heat. Moats are a real danger, especially if covered. Even if they are open, they may extend back under the snow much farther than is obvious, and sometimes are of formidable depth. To a degree, the solution is to give protruding rocks a wide berth. The moats along the bottom of cliffs may, however, be taken advantage of, as they sometimes provide easier and safer climbing than the snow itself.

Many changes in texture can be guessed at according to temperatures and general snow conditions. Others, such as sudden changes from snow to ice, can be determined by probing with the axe. Be constantly on the alert for altered conditions.

Avalanches, Rockfalls, and Cornices

Slopes that are likely to avalanche should of course not be climbed, and must be crossed with extreme caution; but you have to recognize an avalanche slope to avoid it. Masses of avalanching snow may suffocate, crush, or simply bury you without a trace. Snow avalanches are of course much more common in winter and spring than in the latter part of the summer, the normal climbing season. In general, avoid gullies and steep, unbroken slopes that are covered with deep new snow (whether it is wet, dry, or wind-packed), or by large amounts of wet melting snow. Extensive observation and experience should eventually provide a background knowledge of when and where slopes are stable enough to climb, and when and where they can be safely crossed. While gaining this knowledge, avoid couloirs that appear hazardous. Ridges often provide safe alternate routes.

Less obvious, and lasting perhaps through the climbing season, is the possibility of spontaneous rockfall. The danger especially exists on rock faces, or in snow and ice gullies that lie between rock faces, during periods of heavy melting. The evidence of rockfall can be easily seen in gullies of snow and ice. Rocks and dirt may lie on the snow surface, either in the couloir proper or at its foot in a fan. Long vertical grooves in the snow are also evidence of either avalanche or rockfall. The evidence may be concealed by even a light snowfall, which at the same time may add to the danger. Some walls seem to discharge rocks at any time, others only when in the sun. The signs in the snow may tell you which part of the gully is safe to ascend and which part dangerous. A broad couloir is more apt to provide a safe route than is a narrow one.

Cornices are another feature that should be avoided altogether by climbers of limited experience, but should be recognized and understood. Cornices are formed during winter storms on the leeward crests of ridges, especially ridges that have one steep side and one gentle side. They are overhangs of snow shaped almost like ocean waves, gradually built up as winter winds blow snow over the steep drop from the gentle side of the crest. As an inexperienced climber you would presumably never be climbing beneath a cornice's overhanging side, nor try to cut your way through it. But you very well might arrive on a nice broad snow ridge from the easy side, without realizing that the flat area is, in part, hanging unsupported over nothingness on the far side. By observing surrounding ridges, looking for a possible crack line, probing with your axe, and exercising caution, you can avoid getting out on the cornice beyond its probable line of fracture.

Temporary Snow and Ice Conditions

Conditions with which the climber must cope, even though

they are not strictly snow and ice climbing, occur during or after sudden storms. The new snow tends to blow, melt, or fall off steep rocks, while lying inconveniently cold, wet, and slippery on handholds and footholds. Snow which has melted and then frozen, or rain which has frozen, may coat rocks with thin, almost invisible, glassy ice called verglas. Snow, either fresh or melting, may cause avalanches and rockfall in gullies and troughs, or hide the nature of what lies beneath the surface. Such conditions must be dealt with by greatly increased safety measures both in use of equipment and in general attitude.

Glaciers, What and Where

All the problems, conditions, techniques, safeguards, equipment, and clothing that pertain to snow and ice work are also applicable to glacier climbing—and then some! Superficial conditions are much the same for both, but some special conditions of vital importance to climbers are built right into glacier structure.

In simplified form, glaciers may be described as large masses of slowly moving ice that exist as permanent features of mountain architecture. They form and thrive in mountainous or other regions where weather, climate, exposure, elevation, and latitude combine, over long periods of time, to permit enormous accumulations of snow which become compressed into ice. This ice mass slowly moves downhill, melting at its lower margin and being renewed by fresh snow in its upper portions, with the seasons. The transition zone between snow and ice is called firn or névé.

The extent of glaciers varies enormously. One mountain

may be mainly rock, with one small glacier and some snow chutes. Another may be covered almost completely by a vast network of glaciers, perhaps separated by rock ridges in their upper portions and flowing into each other in their lower portions. There are limitless combinations. The surface of a glacier may look like a snowfield. It may be large or small, rough or quite smooth, sparkling with fresh snow or so covered with gravel and dirt that it is hard to believe ice lies underneath. The ice itself is seen late in the year when the snow has melted, in tumbled icefalls or at glacier snouts, or in the deep fissures or crevasses that open in the surface of the slowly moving glacier.

Relation of Glacier Motion to Climbing

The slow but mighty movement of glaciers produces the features that differ from plain snow and ice. Glacier action as affecting climbers may be considered either past and done with, or current and changing.

Past Effects of Glacier Motion

Eons of grinding glaciers (in present or long-ago locations) have, of course, had a monumental role in geological history. Glaciers have carved sheer cliffs, plucked out cirques, polished granite slabs, and deposited huge mounds of ground-up, mixed-up rubble known as moraines, which make good or terrible walking according to shape, composition, and location. These and other effects can be taken for granted as the status quo in any one lifetime.

Contemporary Effects of Glacier Motion

Other results of glacier motion are continuous, current processes—some important, some merely of interest. One by-product of glaciers is the finely ground silt, or "glacier flour" discharged in the melt water. This silt gives the beautiful opaque colors to many high-mountain lakes, and the dense, milky (or dishwatery) appearance to streams originating in glaciers. A glacier river is difficult to ford because you cannot see the bottom. And climbers may think twice before drinking water so full of grit even though it is perfectly harmless, and most of the particles soon settle when the water stands in a cup or pot.

Crevasses and Bergschrunds

For climbers the most vital thing about glaciers is the formation and endless change of crevasses and bergschrunds. As the ice moves over steep or uneven parts of its course, or is forced by the shape of its bed to change direction, splits and cracks form in the ice at or near the surface. These fissures may be narrow cracks or formidable dark caverns hundreds of feet deep. They have shining ice walls or reveal many layers of old ice and dirt. You may hear water running in them, or see enormous icicles festooning their walls. They are sometimes gapingly obvious, and at other times covered securely or insecurely with snow. They are most prevalent at manifestly steep, convex, or irregular sections of the flow. But who can see beneath a glacier? A crevasse may be anywhere; and where there is one, there are often others roughly parallel to it. Where the glacier breaks away from the mountain at or near its upper end, above the névé, an enormous crevasse or series of crevasses forms; this is called the bergschrund. The ever present danger of falling into a crevasse is the main difference between ordinary snow and ice climbing, and glacier travel.

How to Start Glacier Climbing

A climber new to glacier travel—even if he has mastered the fundamentals of snow and ice—should not venture upon a glacier without experienced companions. Build up judgment by paying close attention to your changing and complex environment in the company of knowledgeable climbers. Learn how to plan glacier routes from a distance and close up, to avoid heavily crevassed areas. Heed details of technique that make you a safe member of the party, and take full advantage of the formal or informal instruction offered on your early glacier climbs.

When you have gained experience with such groups, and begin to go out on your own, start with routes reasonably familiar, or at least of known difficulty. Forego obvious and unnecessary complications such as icefalls and unknown routes on unfamiliar peaks, until you have well-founded confidence in your capabilities developed on better-known routes. And always practice established safety measures for glacier travel.

Safety Measures for Glacier Travel

Glacier travel is too varied and complicated for a list of arbitrary "rules," but necessary precautions that will greatly increase the likelihood of your staying (or getting) out of crevasses can be given as a guide.

(1) Wear adequate clothing. Surface temperatures may be summery, but it is always wintertime inside crevasses.

(2) Always rope on glaciers, even on an easy or flat slope. Crevasses can and do exist on flat portions of glaciers, or in sections where they have been previously unknown.

(3) Three on a rope is the preferred number for glacier travel. Two or more ropes traveling together are safer than one.

(4) Always wear the wrist loop of your ice axe; you must not lose it.

(5) Before setting off across a glacier, attach three prusik slings to the rope and stow them in pockets or otherwise out of the way. The middle man should put one of the slings on the rope going to the man behind him. He might be held on either rope, and need a loop to stand in while adjusting the others.

(6) Tie a small loop in the rope a few feet from the waist loop (to anchor a fallen climber with the axe through the loop).

(7) Where ease of climbing permits, travel continuously, the rope fully extended between climbers, and each member of the rope prepared to give a belay instantly if one person falls into a crevasse.

(8) You are not apt to fall into a wide-open crevasse. The danger lies in those hidden beneath a snow surface too weak to bear your weight, especially likely on the névé. Such spots can sometimes be detected by a long trough of slightly depressed snow, or other textural changes. Each climber should

probe the snow surface with his axe; it goes in more readily and deeply if a thin layer of snow over a hole has been reached. When you find one crevasse, suspect others nearby. If possible, walk at right angles to suspected crevasses, and avoid having the entire party over the same crevasse (surprise!).

(9) If a crevasse fall occurs in continuous climbing, throwing yourself into a self-arrest is probably the best way to hold it. Change to consecutive climbing with careful belays when the climbing becomes difficult or any but the most minor crevasse crossing is contemplated.

Crossing Crevasses

All crevasses deserve careful inspection, partly for reasons of their sheer sensational interest, but especially with a view to getting safely to the other side. Consider how serious a fall would be, and how difficult it would be to get out. Some are narrow and shallow, but have slick walls that converge so you could be wedged in tightly. Some are water-filled. Some are so full of snow that a landing might be soft and harmless, but you could fall right through the snow you see. There may be broad ledges near the top, or black depths the eye cannot measure. Some have gentle walls that appear easily climbable; others may be undercut in a "bell" shape that is especially difficult to surmount.

Many crossings can (or must) be avoided, either by laying out a route that bypasses crevasses altogether or makes detours around the ends. A crevasse that is partly or largely snow-covered requires particularly close inspection, as the ends or edges may be unstable. "Bridges" of snow sometimes present the shortest or perhaps the only way to get across but must be inspected carefully from every angle for thickness, stability, and surface cracks that might indicate weakness. When the crossing is to be attempted, set up sound belay spots well away from the edge. The leader should step with care, and test with his axe. On the far side, he should make sure he is well beyond the first crevasse but has not encountered another before setting up his belay. The second and subsequent persons should step gently in the leader's steps (unless he made a hole), and they too should probe. A bridge frozen solid in the morning may be ready to collapse by the return in the afternoon.

Bergschrunds present similar problems, but may be more trouble than other crevasse crossings, in part because they often cannot be avoided. Bergschrunds are often easy to cross early in the season when covered or clogged with snow, especially at one end or the other. Or they may present almost insuperable difficulties late in the season, when the chasm is so pronounced that there is no choice but to climb down into it and out again. Such a maneuver may be unusually difficult because of a much higher, overhanging upper lip. It is sometimes the better part of valor to give up the peak rather than make the bergschrund crossing twice. If you do get across, take special pains not to fall into it from the steep slopes above.

Getting Out of Crevasses

With care (and luck), you have a good chance of never falling into a crevasse at all (few climbers do). If you do fall in, however, the results may vary from trivial to fatal. Some knowledge of how to get out and how to help a fellow climber emerge, greatly enhances the likelihood of survival.

Self-Rescue, Aided by Team

Self-rescue presupposes that you are uninjured or only slightly hurt. It does not imply that your teammates contribute no help. At the very least, a belay gives moral support. It may supply the physical assistance without which self-rescue would be impossible. After falling, assess your position and inform those above. Make sure they have a chance to set up a good belay before you move. If you are on snow or can be lowered to a ledge or snow, move with care to prevent falling further. If you are not wearing all the warm clothing you have with you, put it on at once. You may find an easy exit up outward-sloping walls, or walls close enough together for chimneying. You may have to prusik up the rope. If you are dangling in space, get your weight off the waist loop as soon as you can. Pass one of the pre-arranged prusik slings around the back of one leg and over the foot. Stand in this loop, arrange the remaining prusiks, and ascend quickly before the cold and strain sap your strength.

Team members above should safeguard themselves and each other from falling into the same or other crevasses. They should analyze the terrain, work from the lower lip on steep slopes, and avoid knocking snow or gear onto the victim. The rope will cut back into an overhanging lip of snow; the cutting can be minimized by placing rolled-up clothing or a well-anchored ice axe between the rope and the snow.

A rescue method which is similar, but faster and less strenuous, is the Bilgiri. Its use depends on having an extra rope or an end long enough to serve as an extra rope, with enough people to handle two ropes from above. The second rope is lowered with a loop tied in the end for a footstep. Pass this loop down through your waist loop. Stand in it. Adjust a prusik on your own climbing rope for your other foot, and another to go around your chest. While your weight is on one of the ropes, the climbers above pull up the other a short distance. Transfer your weight to the upper loop. Repeat.

Team Rescue

Injury sustained in a crevasse fall is a very serious matter. The victim may be virtually inaccessible, and is in a bitterly cold place. This is the circumstance where a life may depend on an adequately large party, with at least one member who understands pulley setups for climbing rescues. Without such resources and methods, the injured man can seldom be just pulled out. An inexperienced rope of two or three has little choice but to assess the situation, try to prevent additional injury, and go or send at once for outside help.

If a climbing companion disappears into a crevasse, do not panic; you cannot help by joining him. If there are two or more climbers above, it is reasonably easy to divide up the belaying, investigating, anchoring, etc. If you are alone, and the man cannot get out or even communicate with you, you are in real trouble. However, you *have* to free yourself or eventually fall in too. If at all possible, secure the fallen man with an anchor. One method is to drive an axe deep into the snow through the loop previously placed in your rope. Another method is to attach a sling to the climbing rope with a prusik, and drop it over the axe. You should anchor the victim, whether or not he is hanging free on the rope; but of course it is easier if he has come to rest. If his weight is on the rope and you cannot anchor him without slipping, let him down slowly in the hope that he will land on a ledge or snow bank. (In the really unlikely but terrible circumstance of his still dangling unanchored when all the rope is out, with no one to help, there is probably no choice but for you to try to cut the rope, or fall in too—probably forever.)

When you are free to do so, inspect the accident site. If you can do it safely, enter the crevasse by climbing, rappelling, or prusiking down to one side of the victim (to avoid knocking snow on him). Take what equipment you have, including an axe if available. Examine the injured person, give first aid, dress and pad him in all available clothing. If he is not well secured above, anchor him to his axe, an ice piton, or a bollard chopped in the ice. Even his crampons might be used; they should be removed anyway to keep his feet warmer.

Going for Outside Help

If either an injured or uninjured person is in a crevasse and cannot be extricated, someone must go for help. If it was a two-man rope, you must go alone and should have an ice axe. Mark the accident site as clearly as you can for either ground or air search, by laying expendable equipment and clothing out in a conspicuous pattern that won't look like rocks. If there are two free to move and the terrain is feasible for solo climbing, one person should stay with a victim who is still alive. Fix the general location in mind by landmarks, and compass readings if possible, to avoid needless delays in rescue. If you are very lucky, there may be another climbing team nearby to give assistance. You may have to go clear to a ranger station or sheriff's office, where officials will summon a rescue team. It is important that you speed the rescue by directing them as clearly as possible to the site of the accident, and giving complete information as to what they will probably find.

Crevasses are the most characteristic hazard of glacier climbing. Several other problems, which are encountered elsewhere, are intensified on glaciers. The most important of these are coping with bad weather and keeping track of the route for a safe return. They are interrelated.

Weather Problems on Glaciers

Weather is frequently unstable in the mountains, especially so in glacier regions. The large snow and ice masses attract and create storms. Glaciers provide very little chance of shelter in a storm. Visibility can become extremely poor on large snow surfaces devoid of landmarks. To lessen the chance of being caught in a storm, familiarize yourself with the probable weather in particular areas. Heed forecasts, and don't let wishful thinking obliterate good sense if storms are predicted for your chosen climbing day. Turn back when good or borderline weather turns bad. Just in case, wear adequate clothing, and have extra garments that are warm and dry in the pack, including socks. If a storm hits, put your extra clothes on *before* you get chilled. Unless your feet are really wet, the change of socks can be deferred for a possible night out.

In a snow storm or just a thick fog on glaciers, visibility can quickly drop to nil. A snow expanse in a dense fog exudes a sort of dancing emptiness in which it may be difficult to tell up from down, let alone see your way. It is a wise climber who has made provisions to find his way back.

Marking Return Routes

On glaciers it is frequently important to return exactly the way you came. This may be because of dangers, difficulties, or length of alternate routes; because of crevasses to be avoided or crossed; or because a key spot for leaving the glacier is more easily spotted from below than above. Large white expanses minus landmarks are confusing at best, and can seem hopeless in storm, fog, or darkness. Hence precautionary measures should be taken to help retrace your footsteps.

Literally speaking, this may not be possible. Footsteps and axe holes may remain plain for days; they may never show at all if the surface is icy or pocked with irregularities that uncannily resemble footprints, or they may start out deep and unmistakable, yet disappear shortly in sun or wind.

As in all climbing, all members of the party should habitually observe landmarks, both close and far away, and behind as well as ahead. A compass is valuable if you take an occasional bearing on a landmark. You will at least know the general direction you should take on the return (climbers have become so confused that they came down the opposite sides of peaks). Knowing the direction in which you want to go, you can follow an approximate compass bearing without landmarks by lining it up with two climbers ahead.

A more specific way to mark a route is with "willow wands," cut from bushes, or more usually made in advance from three-foot bamboo garden stakes topped with small red or orange fluorescent banners. The sight of an occasional wand on a featureless route is reassuring. In especially obscure or vital portions of the route, the wands should be stuck into the snow a rope length apart, so when one is located the party can be sure of finding another. Major turns or crevasses can be identified by sticking two wands in the snow. And so, it is hoped, a successful return is made from a successful climb.

Snow, ice, and glacier climbs with experienced companions enable you to build up increasing knowledge, through participation and observation, until you can assume responsibility for yourself and others. Long before this stage—and long after—you will be enjoying complete mountain ascents.

chapter six

Preparing for Mountain Ascents: Planning, Approach, and High Camp

THERE are few climbing areas in North America where climbers can step from their cars and almost immediately rope up for technical ascents. Some rock climbing centers and a few peaks qualify. But most mountaineering involves a long backpack to establish a high camp from which the peak itself can be climbed in one day.

Besides technical climbing skills, considerable information and preparation go into successful ascents of big peaks. The full scope of a complete mountain ascent and descent can be roughly divided into several stages: planning, preparation, approach and high camp, ascent, descent to camp, and packing out.

Planning a Climb

Detailed planning of all phases of a climb is important to safety, success, and enjoyment. An inexperienced member of an experienced party, whether it be club or private enterprise, may not realize the amount of planning done before a climb. Experienced members in charge have often made so many ascents that the planning they do is automatic and inconspicuous. One reason for laying plans is the interrelationship of many aspects of a climb; another is to make sure that everyone has everything along that will be really needed.

Selection of Peak and Route

The decision of what to climb is based on a number of things, including accessibility, the time available, whim, suitability, and appeal for the particular climbers. The choice is sometimes made because the area is new or is a favorite. Details not already known can be learned from other climbers, climbers' guidebooks, and Forest Service and topographical maps. Except for miles of backpacking, climbers seldom refer to distances. Pertinent statistics are given in elevations, elevation gains, and approximate hours.

Selection of Climbing Party

Club climbs are usually scheduled long ahead of time, and supervised by leaders who are familiar with the area and who have the knowledge and authority to limit participation to those qualified. Such regulations are based on safety. Requirements differ from club to club, and are fairly flexible; if you are new in a group, inquire. Leaders of club climbs are chosen for their ability to make decisions and cope with problems. Under such tutelage, an interested novice can gain experience quickly and safely.

Private climbing parties should apply similar though informal principles in their own choice of personnel. They have more leeway, in that they can tailor the party to suit the climb—or the climb to suit the experience and physical fitness of the party.

The traditional number to provide a margin of safety is a minimum of three or four. Too large a group may be awkward to keep track of, and dangerous on routes where loose rock is common. A party of two, or a solo climber, must accept and compensate for the risks of having no back-up party. They should stay within their established climbing abilities, and exercise a high degree of caution and care. The disadvantages of a small number are at times offset by the pleasures of privacy and solitude, or the speed and efficiency of a well-matched pair.

Choice of Clothing and Climbing Equipment

When information has been assembled about approach and climb, clothing and needed climbing equipment can be selected. Clothing for high mountain ascents, even on rock routes, will be similar to that listed under snow and ice climbing because of temperatures and weather conditions at high elevations. Mountaineering boots are usually essential, and are customarily worn on rock in preference to carrying kletterschuhe to remote areas.

Ropes, pitons, and carabiners are "group" items, and the weight should be parceled out. One summit pack for at least every two people is minimum. Hammers, ice axes, and crampons are individual responsibilities. If you are not sure what you should take, ask. In choosing equipment, keep in mind that at high elevations, or in poor weather, routes are more difficult than they are at sea level. It will not do to run short on things you really need, but climbing gear is so heavy that you cannot take an unlimited amount of it "just in case."

Much of the planning and preparation involves the same problems whether the outing is for two days or two weeks. But the farther the climbers go from civilization and the longer they intend to stay, the more they need certain things. These include the knowledge and equipment to avoid trouble, or to cope with it if it comes.

Mishaps and Emergencies

Accidents in the mountains are rare among mountaineers who understand and cater to their environment and their own abilities. Dangers which are environmental are considered "objective" dangers: storms, lightning, crevasses, falling rocks, and other natural conditions over which the climber has no direct control. Hazards created at least in part by the climber himself are called "subjective" dangers: poor judgment, overconfidence, slips, inadequate preparation, lack of proper physical conditioning, illness, and the like. Learning over a period of time to understand, forecast, avoid, or deal with potential hazards greatly increases the safety and satisfaction of mountaineering.

Several specific things not already mentioned can be done at home to increase your competence on trips. Be sure to:

(1) Keep in good physical condition.
(2) Study first aid, with particular attention to lacerations,

bleeding, head and spinal injuries, dislocations, broken bones, frostbite, and shock.

(3) Learn at least rudimentary techniques for rescues. Many climbing clubs arrange or give instruction and practice in rescue techniques.

Safety Precautions on Trips

In connection with specific trips and general attitudes for all trips in the mountains, the following additional points are suggested for helping to keep out of trouble:

(1) For each trip, leave detailed word of your itinerary and the latest possible time of return with someone who will really notice if you do not come back. Write down the information, including the name of a climbing friend, ranger station, or sheriff to notify. Those at home should never really worry if a party is a few hours or even a day overdue, as minor delays are common.

(2) Have extra supplies in the car: water, food, and spare clothing and shoes.

(3) Carry first aid supplies. Since the personnel of your climbing group varies from trip to trip, have your own and make sure a kit is carried on your rope. It should be stocked with mild antiseptic; aspirin and salt tablets; codeine or other pain-killing drugs prescribed by a physician; adhesive tape, gauze bandages, and sterile gauze pads; a single-edge razor blade or a small pair of scissors that cut; elastic bandage for sprains, and a splint (at least above timberline). The most compact and adaptable type of splint is made of hardware cloth; it must be well padded in use. Waterproof

matches, pencil, paper, and safety pins might be added.

(4) Make it a habit to notice your surroundings (and companions).

(5) Use common sense. In bad weather, stay in camp or turn back from a climb when it becomes obvious that you should.

(6) If you suddenly or gradually feel absurdly listless, or nauseated, at elevations from about 10,000 feet on up, suspect altitude sickness, which is caused by shortage of oxygen. It may be cured by rest, deep breathing, and a little easily digested food. A "motion sickness" drug seems to help some people. Recovery may be spontaneous and quick, or not arrive until you descend. Keep in good physical condition as an aid to prevention. A sudden dry cough with no apparent cause may be the beginning of the rare but serious pulmonary edema. Breathing difficulty may follow. The victim should be assisted to a lower elevation at once.

(7) In minor accidents, make every effort to help yourself, or to assist a member of your party, rather than calling for help. For instance, a person with a broken arm might easily walk out after splinting it, resting, and taking a pain-killer, if others carry his pack. Outside rescue is time-consuming, expensive, and if unneeded, is an imposition on others.

Trouble the Party Cannot Cope with

If you think self-rescue may compound an injury, or if a major accident occurs, you must get outside help. Keep your head; the first thing to do in an accident is to figure out how to help the injured person if it can be done. Get him to a safe place. Give him first aid. Try to keep any open wound clean.

Someone must go for help, even if the victim is dead. The fastest assistance will come if there are other climbers in the vicinity. Climbing parties usually are alert to trouble on another rope nearby. Otherwise, contact a ranger station or sheriff's office. Those going for help must use care, especially if they are quite upset. Complete information (preferably written down so none of it is forgotten) should cover the location of the accident, the condition of the victim, and what help is needed. In most major climbing areas, there are nearby volunteer or official rescue groups who have the manpower, training, and experience to respond quickly and efficiently. Helicopters are frequently used to speed rescue, and radios to correlate all operations.

As to the victim, bend all efforts toward keeping him alive until help comes. If he must be left alone on steep terrain, tie him on very securely. It is much better not to leave an injured or disabled person all alone, as his judgment is often impaired. If the party is large enough, get a sleeping bag for him from camp. Provide water and food. Try to keep up his morale; it may be a long wait. Mishaps that might be easily dealt with under city conditions are often greatly magnified by the time and distance before help can arrive in the mountains.

Backpacking and Camping Equipment for Climbers

Camping equipment for long rugged trips must be light and sturdy, and kept to a minimum. Things really needed are discussed.

Packframe

Any old packboard will do for initial trips, but do not try to carry a heavy load in a rucksack. A well-designed pack-frame is needed for frequent pack-ins. The best are of tubular aluminum, with nylon fittings, and a waist strap that permits a balanced load supported largely on the hips. Climbers of your acquaintance can recommend a good brand which will serve your needs. It will be expensive but durable. Choose the right size for your build. It should be fitted with a good-sized sack that will hold a big load and has outer pockets for things needed on the trail.

Sleeping Bag

Nights in climbing camps are often cold. A good down bag is the only kind that is sufficiently warm, light, and compact. A medium-priced bag with two to three pounds of prime goose down (color unimportant) will keep you warm. A mummy-case design that tapers at head and foot makes the most efficient use of the down. You may prefer a more roomy bag with a drawstring at the top, but it must be long enough to cover your head. The lightest material for the casing is rip-stop nylon. Seams should be of box or over-lapping-tube construction, not sewn through. The zipper should be heavy duty, and insulated with a baffle. Sleeping bags are usually crammed into stuff bags for backpacking, and should be shaken up well before use on cold nights. They should be stored loose between trips to keep the down fluffy.

Mattress

To save weight, you can sleep directly on the ground (except, of course, for a ground sheet). If you wish comfort while saving time and trouble, take a mattress. Two feet by four feet is big enough; clothing and equipment go under head and feet. Air mattresses are resilient and compact, but often leak. A pad of plastic foam such as urethane, an inch and a half thick, or thinner if one can be found, is very comfortable. The material is absorbent and should have a waterproof cover; it is light but somewhat bulky. Ensolite pads about a quarter or a half inch thick are waterproof, compact, and excellent insulation (for sleeping on snow, for instance), but are not very soft.

Shelter

Climbers usually take along some sort of shelter, no matter how sketchy. A plastic tube about nine feet long and three feet in diameter can be pitched anywhere you can rig a ridgeline. Equipment or rounded stones placed inside hold down the edges. Its main disadvantage is condensation inside. Another lightweight type of shelter is made from a coated nylon tarp, or a sheet of plastic such as a painter's drop cloth. It should be about nine by twelve feet. Do not forget cord for pitching.

A lightweight tent with a rain fly is desirable or necessary in areas and seasons of heavy precipitation and cold wind. A tent also keeps out insects and affords privacy. A good backpacking tent is a considerable monetary investment, and should be selected with care. Consult other tent owners about how satisfactory theirs have been as to water repellency, material, and design. Never buy a tent without first pitching it yourself (it may be a hopelessly awkward procedure). Consider size, shape, weight, height, poles, etc., in the light of your own preferences.

Except for one-man tubes, shelters are considered group equipment to save weight; such arrangements are made before a trip.

Personal and Miscellaneous Equipment

Various miscellaneous items should be taken on every trip. Some should be carried by each climber, in his pack or his pockets, and some are considered group equipment.

Individual Miscellany

This includes dark glasses or goggles; pocketknife; sunburn preventive and lip salve; insect repellent; cheap pocket watch (climbing is hard on wrist watches); toilet paper (in pocket and pack—lots); handkerchief; band-aids; things for taping up sore spots on feet (adhesive tape, moleskin, and lamb's wool to protect blisters); needle, thread, and safety pins; toilet articles (toothbrush, comb, metal or other small mirror, towel, soap; and for women, some et ceteras); personal prescription drugs.

Group or Individual Miscellany

These articles may be individual or community equipment, according to wish and weights: camera and film; route information; maps and compass; flashlight with alkali batteries (reverse one battery to prevent drain of juice if the switch is accidentally turned on in the pack); plastic or aluminum water bottle; folding pocket cup (sometimes you cannot get at water without one); pencil and paper; first aid kit.

Cooking Equipment

Climbers often like to cook individually, except on longer trips where several may cook together to save the weight of duplicate equipment. Supplies are about the same either way, except that the size of the pots has to be adapted to the number they serve. A one-quart and a quart-and-a-half size are about right for two or three. Keep dishes to a minimum.

Necessary Cooking Equipment

Pots, two (cheap aluminum kettles, with metal or bail handles—or use a gripper); covers, one or two (they hasten cooking, and can double as frying pans or plates); wooden matches (some in waterproof container in pocket, many in pack); cups, one apiece (aluminum, enamel, or plastic); spoons, one apiece (dessert or tablespoon size); rags or paper towels (to use as pot holders, dish towels, etc.).

Optional Cooking Equipment

Can opener, midget G.I. or roll type; cloth sack for sooty pots; fire-starting aids (newspapers, candle, chemical fuel tablets); container for carrying water a long distance to camp (collapsible plastic water bottle or large canteen);

stove, one-burner pressure type; extra fuel for stove (liquid fuel must be carried in a special can with filters and a tight cap).

Stoves versus Fires

Whether to cook on a stove or over a wood fire depends on camping conditions and personal preference. Wood saves weight, is in keeping with the surroundings, and if camp is below timberline is the obvious choice. If you plan on open fires, find out beforehand from the Forest Service if a fire permit is required. Climbers never carry a woodsman's axe, but rely on dead wood (sometimes ridiculously scarce in much-used campsites). Build your fire on sand or rock (*not* on humus), and well away from logs and trees. Construct a simple rock fireplace just wide enough so the pots can span the rocks, and just high enough to allow a good draft without raising the pans out of reach of the flames. A quite small fire is adequate for cooking.

Take a small one-burner stove, if the weather is apt to be cold and wet; if you want to cook in the tent; if you don't like to fool with fires or get your pots sooty; to help insure a hot breakfast *and* a quick start on climbing mornings; and, of course, if you plan to camp above timberline. Several brands and types of stoves are sold in mountaineering shops. Consider weight, screening from wind, likelihood of tipping over, and apparent ease of lighting. Some burn white (unleaded) gasoline, some kerosene, and some butane gas in cylinders (convenient, but troublesome in cold weather). Extra fuel must usually be carried. Keep gasoline and kerosene away from the food in the pack (their flavor lacks taste-appeal). Be sure you can operate the stove before you try it at high camp. When it has not been used for some time, check it to see if it still works. One small stove can cook efficiently for only three or four at the very most.

Food

Food is the one thing you take that increases in amount for every day away from a source of supply. For this reason and others it must be chosen with care. Climbing leaves scant time and energy for cooking—and even scant interest in it when appetites grow delicate with altitude and exhaustion. High camp conditions frequently fall short of ideal for meal preparation, what with crotchety fires or stoves, skimpy fuel supplies, icy water, cold wind, and low boiling points (water boils at 198 degrees at 7500 feet, at 194 degrees at 10,000 feet, etc.). Although an occasional enthusiast declares that climbing and gourmet cooking can and should co-exist, they usually do not.

Types and Amounts of Food to Take

Take food you like. Make sure it is quick and simple to prepare and eat. It should be largely dehydrated, concentrated in bulk and food value, durable, and proof against spoilage. Cooking time roughly doubles with every 5000 feet of elevation, but anything supposed to cook at a "simmer" in a few minutes ought to be satisfactory. Include foods that can be eaten uncooked in an emergency, or just warmed up.

Individual needs vary as to daily amounts of food. Teen-agers and other bottomless eaters can consume two or more pounds of concentrated, dehydrated foods per man-day, and still be ravenously hungry. Light eaters can perhaps get by on one pound per man-day. Average eaters find a pound and a half satisfactory, or at least all they want to carry.

If you want to know how many calories this amount of concentrated food will provide, you can figure it out roughly by allowing 200 calories per ounce for foods that are mostly fat, and 100 calories per ounce for foods that are mostly proteins and carbohydrates. More important, perhaps, is how your digestive system reacts to them. Some fat is desirable, but it often seems hard to digest under climbing conditions. Proteins digest more readily than fats, and "stick to the ribs" longer than carbohydrates. Carbohydrates (starch and sugar) are easiest to digest and provide quick energy. Among suitable climbing foods, about 20 per cent of the calories should come from fats, 30 to 40 per cent from proteins, and 40 to 50 per cent from carbohydrates (most foods are a mixture). This proportion will provide roughly 4500 calories in two pounds of food for backpacking. An active person needs between 3000 and 5000 calories a day. It hardly seems worth figuring out for a few days. Forget calories, consider total weights, take a few vitamin pills if you want to, and eat heartily when you get back home.

Menu Planning and Groceries

For short trips of two or three days, take anything you want to, as long as you are sure it will not subject you to food poisoning. For longer trips, detailed pre-planning of meals and a little rationing on the trip are necessary to be reasonably sure the food will come out even. Make a list of prospective campsites and the elevations. Consider the method of cooking, the activities planned, the personal tastes and the appetite of each person. Make out a menu for every single meal. From the menu list, make your grocery list. Include plenty of salt, as you may crave salt to replace that lost through body dehydration. Take a little extra food for emergencies. Keep your lists (with notations added after the trip) for future reference. Satisfactory meals for climbing trips can be made up from the following suggestions.

Breakfasts. Start active days with small breakfasts. Large ones are time-consuming to prepare, and most climbers find a full stomach a serious liability. A satisfactory climbing breakfast can include stewed fruit (cooked the day before); cold or "instant" hot cereal, with sugar and dried milk; a hot beverage such as cocoa, instant coffee, or tea bags boiled for a few minutes (purists may shudder, but remember that at high elevations the traditional "full rolling boil" is hardly as hot as sea-level steeping). Provide a few hearty, time-consuming breakfasts for days in camp—dried scrambled eggs, bacon, pancakes and brown-sugar syrup.

Lunches. Instead of one large lunch, eat a series of snacks all day long on trail or climb. Keep some lunch food in your pocket, so you can eat when you want to. Lunch foods are usually bread or crackers, cheese, hard sausage, jerky, nuts, raisins, fig bars, candy (some hard—lemon drops are good), and lemonade mix or instant iced tea. Some climbers put everything (except the beverages) all together in a sack and let it integrate.

Dinners. Quickest and easiest to cook and eat are one-pot concoctions. Start with an appropriate amount of water. Add a dried soup mix for flavor, and thickening and nutritional agents as desired or available: macaroni, cheese, sausage, potato powder, canned meat or fish, instant rice, chipped beef, noodles, margarine, and seasonings. Many of these ingredients can be served separately for variety, or eaten as-is when cooking becomes impossible. Dried fruits, well sweetened, can be cooked after the main meal, and it is just as well to cook some up for a few meals ahead. Cookies make good desserts. Margarine, which keeps better than butter, contributes the day's fat. More complicated dinners can be fixed on rest days; try out some of the freeze-dried vegetables and meats (what a miracle to see pieces of cardboard turn into beefsteaks and pork chops!), make instant puddings, etc.

Where to Buy Climbing Foods

Suitable foods can be obtained from several sources. Sporting goods stores carry well-packaged dehydrated and freeze-dried foods. (Some of these can also be ordered through the mail.) Dehydrated scrambled eggs and freeze-dried meats are not readily available elsewhere. Most other foods of this type are easy to find at supermarkets, and are less expensive there. Modern supermarkets carry a wide variety of dehydrated food; just look for it. It may be easier to find the "dry" cheeses that resist melting in special cheese stores, but any natural cheese is satisfactory (processed cheeses spoil). Usually only bakeries sell unsliced bread, which stays fresh longer and usually holds together better than sliced.

Repackaging and Protecting Food

After buying the food, repackage it. Commercial containers are often bulky and heavy but give little protection. Plastic sacks closed with string or rubber bands protect food from moisture. Label the bags as to contents, and put in any needed directions. Margarine can be carried in a screw-top can. Food already put up in plastic bags or foil envelopes should be kept that way, but grouped inside plastic sacks. Cereals, powdered coffee, salt, and sugar may need an inner cloth sack to prevent disaster in case of a puncture. While you are on the move, it is handy to have the food sorted by meals. For camp, it is usually adequate to bag things by category.

In camp, food needs some extra care. Things that should be kept cool can be placed in the shade, immersed in the stream, or buried in snow. Put a good rock on a covered kettle of food. Plastic sacks are theoretically rainproof, but they often develop holes and should be stored under the shelter when you leave camp. High-elevation rodents such as ground squirrels, pikas, and porcupines may ignore your food or just love it. If depredations are severe, put all food in a stuff bag and hang it as high as you can. If bears are around, hang it *very* high. You might need it more than they do.

Approach and High Camp

The number of things to take, for high camp and climb, seems a little overwhelming at first, but it all consolidates. To insure remembering everything, keep a detailed list. Check your list before every trip. You can't believe until it happens how easily you can forget the most obvious things (boots, matches, sleeping bag). To simplify trip preparation, store as much gear as you can in the same place. Time is saved if packs are made up as completely as possible at home.

Backpacking Pace

Start up the trail slowly; your second wind will come, and the pack may even seem lighter after a while. You cannot dawdle on long approaches, but to hurry is folly. You can go only as fast as lungs and legs permit—a speed that varies from person to person and depends on such factors as physical condition, trail condition, and elevation. The most efficient pace is one you can maintain for hours with an occasional pause to get your breath and a few longer rests to eat, drink, and enjoy the view. Excessively long rests waste time and make it hard to re-establish an efficient pace. A determined slogging will take you farther, sooner, than spurts and collapses. Keep your mind on the surroundings instead of on sore feet.

Terrain Problems on the Approach

A trail is the easiest approach, and sometimes goes clear to high camp. Don't leave it until you must. At some point, the party usually takes off across rough, steep, cross-country going. From here on, keep in touch with each other. Take the most open, brush-free route you can find. Cross streams with caution. Look for narrow places that can be safely jumped, stepping stones, log bridges, or broad shallow fords. Wading in your boots is safer than going barefoot. If the stream is dangerous, the first and last men must be roped;

other members can cross with either a fixed handline or a belay. If you do not have an ice axe with you, use a strong pole for balance. Glacier streams are lower in the mornings than in the afternoons.

Reaching Selected Campsite

On a three-day trip, the first day is usually spent packing in, the second climbing, and the third packing out. On longer trips, several days may be devoted to backpacking. In either case, the selected campsite is a fairly inflexible goal. For a particular climb, it may be a traditional spot. For a new route or seldom-made ascent, the general camping location is chosen for its proximity to the climb. Study maps, calculate route length and difficulty, consult others, and inspect the terrain from a distance; then find the exact place on arrival.

High Camp Requisites

Basic requirements for a climbing camp are few—just water, sleeping spots, and fuel if you are counting on firewood.

Water, of course, is necessary. A stream, lake, or tarn is best, even if the water must be carried some distance. A trickle or drip from a snowbank can be collected in pots. The source may freeze up overnight, so fill all containers in the afternoon or evening (and on freezing nights take the canteen to bed). Snow can be melted over the fire, but this takes time, toil, and fuel. Sometimes liquid is manufactured during daylight hours by spreading snow on a dark poncho; but alas, the results are not water, only poncho juice.

Sleeping sites have to be found where the shelter or tent can be set up. For individual beds, a very small flat spot is adequate; for several to use the same shelter, a bigger place is needed. Flat places can be enlarged by building up edges and leveling humps. Remove major rocks from the bed. Give attention to drainage, both natural and by ditching. Your axe is a splendid digging and prying tool, but don't break the handle. The location of your bedsite may help you keep warm. Look for a spot which is a little above streams and meadows and a little sheltered on the uphill side, since cold air flows downhill. A built-up or natural windbreak is helpful, and dry ground is warmer than wet (although sleeping on snow is more comfortable than it sounds). To erect tubes or shelters, string a ridge line from boulders or trees. Shelters can be put up in a multitude of designs. Tie the corners and sides firmly to rocks or bushes. If there are no grommets, tie the cords tightly around little bunches of the plastic. Pitch shelters tautly to cut down on their whipping in the wind. Plastic will cut easily, and cuts should be mended promptly with adhesive tape. It is easier to pitch a tent above timberline than a shelter, as poles eliminate the need for other support. A tent is warm enough so that meadow camping is feasible. Frequent readjustment of all shelters is necessary to keep them tightly pitched.

Firewood is often available among the scattered trees found well above the real forest. Scattered bits of wood are all you need to cook with, and burn well when dry. In wet weather, fires can be slow and time-consuming, and require much craftiness and blowing. Hunt for dry wood under logs or rocks, and use dead dry branches hanging on trees.

Margarine, bacon grease, pitch, and any litter made of rubber (such as old tennis shoes) are supplementary fire starters.

After an arduous approach, you are now established in an austere, beautiful high camp. All this, and heaven too: you will climb tomorrow.

chapter seven

Climbing and Descending
The Peaks

ON a full mountain ascent, the techniques and judgments you have previously learned meld together, and you gain in climbing maturity on each climb. Every ascent differs from every other. None turns out exactly as planned. But there is a similarity of pattern in both success and disaster that establishes the wisdom of knowing what you are about. Your immediate goal is reaching the summit. Getting there and back safely and with finesse is competent mountaineering.

Preparations the Night before the Climb

You usually start getting ready for the following day's climb as soon as the climbing camp is established.

Making Up the Ropes

A club or large private party usually camps where several

peaks or various routes are accessible. Avoid having more than one or two ropes on the same route, especially on rock, where parties cannot spread out for efficient travel and for protection from loose rocks. The group leaders consult individuals as to wishes and abilities; ropes are made up so each includes a leader equal to the route and others to round out a safe party. If two ropes are to be on the same climb, the strongest and fastest goes first. Small private parties, of course, have already chosen the rope members and the route.

Studying Routes

If the route is unfamiliar or somewhat indefinite, and is visible from camp or from a high point nearby, it should be studied and restudied by the entire party. A closer inspection, and often a view from a new angle, is obtained of the general line to the summit. Note key points along the route, step-by-step details, and possible alternatives going either up or down. These factors are often hard to assess when you are on the route, due to foreshortening.

Planning the Departure Time

For all but the shortest climbs and the most experienced parties, plan to start early. Climbs have a way of taking the entire day, and even more. You should plan to arise as soon as you can see, or even earlier so as to leave camp as early as visibility permits. An hour usually elapses between getting up and leaving camp. Also calculate how many hours will probably elapse between departure and return. Some of the elements to consider are the length of the climb in elevation gain; the altitude itself; what proportions of the climb are technical and non-technical; overall difficulty; how long it has taken previous parties (and who they were); and the size, speed, and condition of the present party, especially the slowest person. In general, experienced climbers are faster than neophytes on technical work, and a small group is faster than a big one. Allow extra time for stops and for the unexpected. Roughly half of the ascent time should be allowed for the descent.

An exceptionally early start is sometimes advisable due to other conditions. For instance, an established weather pattern of afternoon storms in the area may make it desirable to complete the route before they are due. It is not unusual to set forth on a glacier climb around midnight, as sometimes a portion of the route must be covered before the sun strikes it, or afternoon snow conditions may promise to be particularly bad.

Getting back to camp early in the day does no harm; in fact, it is a delight. Returning in time to cook dinner before dark is highly desirable. Being caught out in complete darkness is inconceivably time-consuming, and sometimes stops you (cold!)

Organizing for the Climb

The bare necessities that must be left till morning take quite long enough; do all you can the night before. Make up your pack, putting in everything not needed overnight (add the rest next morning). Include climbing equipment, food, maps, flashlight, first aid kit, water bottle, extra clothing, dry socks in a plastic bag, and camera (if desired). Remove odds and ends from your pockets, and put things in that you will need in the early morning and on the climb: sunburn dope, lip balm, dark glasses, knife, handkerchief, compass, mittens, watch, toilet paper, band-aids, folding cup.

If you plan to leave a note in camp regarding your route, write it. Sort out the breakfast things, and put the rest of the food away. Sleeping in part of your clothing makes getting up a little less obnoxious. Go to bed early. After a long backpack, insomnia is unlikely, and bed is the best place to keep warm.

Early Morning Preparations

There is always one dependable (but unpopular) climber who wakes up by the appointed hour and rouses the others. Before getting up, inspect the weather. Storm, or clearly impending storm, rules out climbing. Good or indecisive weather compels you to arise. A climb is often approached in uncertain weather that turns out to be beautiful before the technical part is reached. The atmosphere around camp is usually silent and gloomy before dawn as climbers groggily perform their chores; the thought of climbing may seem distasteful or even ominous at that hour.

When to Stay in Camp

Weather influences the plans of the whole party. Indisposition is a personal matter, though it may indirectly affect your friends. If you are really ill, do not go; even using willpower, you could not fail to be a liability on the climb. If you just "don't feel very good," say so but start out; very often you recover after an hour or so. If not, you can turn back alone while still on easy ground close to camp, but not trying to go may cause regret.

Leaving Camp in Order

To make sure of finding all in good order when you return to camp, leave it so. Put all food away. Leave sleeping bags loosely rolled under the shelter and on top of the mattresses. If you have only a ground sheet, roll everything up in that and weight the wad down with rocks. Place rocks on odds and ends such as spoons and soap and anything that might blow away or be carried off by industrious varmints.

Identifying Campsite

Your camp may be so distinctively situated that you can spot it even from the summit. Or it may merge into the landscape. Each climber should fix its location firmly in his mind in relation to major landmarks, tree line, stream courses, etc. Further, when leaving camp, construct one or more unmistakable cairns at conspicuous spots to indicate that camp is near. Look back from time to time and implant its location in your mind.

Terrain Between Camp and Roping-up Point

From high camp there is usually an extension of the approach before roped climbing begins. This may be over meadows, moraines, easy slabs, snow-filled basins and chutes, and increasingly steep slopes of tumbled talus blocks.

Talus

These slopes consist of rock fragments which have piled up below cliffs, usually in gullies that fan out at the bottom. The blocks often start at about house or car size, and as you climb diminish to fist or pea size. The larger pieces are usually well consolidated (but watch out for the occasional rocker); the smaller ones on steep slopes tend to be very loose. Nimble leaping and long steps are required for the first; use your axe for balance or feel, but keep the loop off your wrist. On the loose parts, choose the better consolidated sections if you can. The axe is helpful as a staff. Adjacent snow slopes are generally far preferable to the talus unless they are too icy for the equipment you have available. A route along the foot of the cliff, where you can use occasional handholds, is often easier than the center of the gully. On loose talus where occasional rocks roll down in spite of reasonable care, the group should spread out horizontally so no one is directly below another person. If this is impossible, they should keep close together so falling rocks cannot gain momentum.

Pace

As when backpacking, the climber should not push himself to go faster than breathing and leg muscles permit. Leg movements and breathing do not always coincide on steep going, as momentum is often necessary for a smooth move, with a pause to catch your breath after making the move. A slow start does not mean you will be slow all day, but increasing elevation naturally imposes limitations on speed. Each climber should proceed at his own optimum rate on non-

technical ground, but the faster ones should be sure to keep
in touch with the slower ones.

Rests

Usually the first hour requires a pause to tighten boot
laces, remove surplus garments, etc. When the sun comes
up, another rest is justified for putting on sunburn goop and
dark glasses. Within a couple of hours, the first lunch will
be needed. Tank up on water at every opportunity, as it is
likely to be scarce or absent later. Be sure to fill the water
bottle before you run out of streams. Use each stop to scan
whatever you can see of the route. Make all stops brief. The
extra hours may be badly needed at the end of the day.

Roping Up

The real climb begins when you rope. From now on, you are
not climbing as separate individuals but as a team, each
responsible for himself and the others.

When to Rope

Obviously the rope is needed when steep and exposed
cliffs begin, or when the party steps out on a glacier. Less
obviously, you should rope for borderline rocks which may
be fairly easy, but are so loose or so exposed that a slip could
not be stopped. If you want to tie on before the others do,
say so; it is false pride to climb unroped if you feel insecure.

Reorganizing Equipment

At the roping-up point, arrange all equipment for technical

climbing. On climbs where all ice and snow ends at the point where rock work begins, cache crampons and axes in a spot where they will be protected from falling rocks, such as under a slight overhang; ascertain that they cannot fall off, and be sure you can find them on the way back. If they will be needed above, take them along.

Carrying the Ice Axe on Rock

The axe is sure to be an awkward object to carry while rock climbing. No matter what you do with it, it gets in the way. If it will be unused for long stretches, attach it to the back of the rucksack or stow it head-down in the sack. If the axe will be needed intermittently, stick it through your waist loop, belt, or pack straps (beware of removing the pack before the axe!). Or let it hang from your wrist by the wrist loop, and ignore it as it scrapes along. While you are belaying, lay it carefully aside if it will be safe.

The Technical Climb

The climbing itself, whether on rock, snow, or both, is essentially what you have been doing in practice areas. Psychologically it differs because it is part of a larger enterprise. The remoteness of your location heightens the sense of adventure, independence, and accomplishment. It also demands sharpened techniques, caution, and attention to natural surroundings. Several features of high-mountain conditions differ, at least in emphasis, from those in more accessible climbing areas.

Continuous Climbing on Rock

Easy and more difficult climbing often alternate on intricate high-mountain routes. After the rope is put on, it is usually removed only for very long easy stretches. On portions that do not require a belay, except perhaps for reasons of exposure, the climbers remain roped but all climb at the same time. The leader holds one or two coils in his hand. The second and third are each responsible for the rope in front of them. They coil enough so there are ten to fifteen feet between climbers. Each must be considerate in adapting his pace to that of the others on terrain of uneven difficulty. The climbing may be such that a slip could occur but could be easily held by the others' immediately bracing themselves to take the minor shock. If one climber wants an upper belay, he should request the man ahead to stop and take up rope.

Route Finding

Routes in practice areas often are rigidly defined and become very familiar. On far peaks, where routes are not well known and have many variations, the rope leader must find the way to the summit and also choose among alternative pitches. Sometimes considerable scouting is required to locate a key pitch. If possible, the leader should stay well within the climbing capacities of everyone on the rope.

Loose Rock

In popular rock climbing areas, the rock is generally good to begin with, and over the years most loose chunks have been removed by assiduous "gardening." The high mountains always have some loose rock, usually a lot, and sometimes so much that you wonder how they stand at all. You must learn to climb on or over it without sending fusillades down on those below or losing your own balance. Step fastidiously on ledges. Keep an eye on the rope. Move chunks lying in especially precarious positions, and lay them carefully in more secure places. Choose your belay stances to avoid being in the line of fire from the climbing route. Test all holds, first gingerly and then more firmly. In climbing past an especially unstable rock, avoid even touching it. Learn which loose holds can stand certain pressures without being dislodged, and which are adequate for balance in conjunction with firmer holds.

Climbing Miseries

Rock climbing in particular is usually pursued most ardently under pleasant conditions. When climbing on high peaks, you must be prepared to suffer cheerfully through quite an array of discomforts. You are nearly always either too hot or too cold. Temperatures vary radically with the wind and from sun to shade. Rock climbing in gloves is almost impossible, so expect to climb part of the time with cold hands; wear mittens or gloves for belaying. Between the dry mountain air and lack of water, thirst may be acute. Drink any water you come to, eat available snow and icicles, and stuff snow into your water bottle before it is empty. Otherwise, forget your thirst—until the moment after the climb when you come to that first welcome stream. Huffing and puffing and a touch of malaise are normal; ignore them. The glorious surroundings, and the concentration required

by the climbing, help to keep your mind off your troubles.
The hours fly by. Eventually you reach the top.

The Summit

Summits have great individuality. They range from mild-
looking snow humps to soaring pinnacles. The true summit
of a peak is nearly always marked with a cairn (if not, perhaps
you have realized the climber's dream: a first ascent). Usually
there is a register in which to record your arrival. It may be
anything from a rusty tobacco can to an imposing cast-
aluminum box placed by a climbing club. The ideal summit
includes warm sunshine, a far view in every direction, and
plenty of time to relax, eat, study the map, and read the
register with its comments both historic and funny. True,
not all are ideal; and in any event, watch the time and the
weather. You are on top of the mountain, but the climb is
just half over; you must return to camp.

Turning Back before Reaching Summit

Though all your plans and efforts have been focused on
reaching the top of the mountain, it occasionally becomes
manifest that you must turn back before reaching your goal.
Such decisions are the responsibility of the leader; but
mountain climbing (except with guides) is pretty democratic.
The leader is apt to consult his companions, who usually
feel free and eager to express opinions whether consulted or
not. A rope *must* stay together, even if there is disagreement.
On a technical climb no one should ever be left alone or

leave the party, although two ropes of recognized competence can make independent decisions.

There are several major reasons for not completing an ascent.

Time

When you compare the length of time the climb has taken you with the estimated time for the descent, it may be evident that you must turn back short of the top if you are to get off the difficult portion by dark. Too late a start, a slow party, photography, lingering for fun, and miscalculation are among reasons for running out of time.

Weather

Do your best to predict the weather before going into an area, especially in ranges noted for bad weather. Consider the weatherman's five-day forecasts (for what they are worth). Find out what you can about weather patterns in unfamiliar ranges by asking for local opinions. As mountains attract and make their own weather, *look* long and hard at the sky during the day. The approach of unquestionably bad weather is a good reason to turn back. Rain and snow make both climbers and climbing conditions miserable, and can be dangerous. Lightning in particular is a strong incentive for getting below peaks and ridges with all speed consistent with safety.

Illness and Injury

Real illness from altitude or other cause, while rare,

necessitates descent while the victim can still travel. A minor accident which might have both a physical and a psychological effect is often a good reason for retreat. If there is plenty of time and the weather is good, the party can rest and think it over before the final decision is made.

The Descent

Descending is easier and faster than going up because you are not working against gravity. But there are problems as well as advantages. The party usually retraces the route of ascent, except when there is a familiar route that is known to be easier. If the first man down is not sure of the route, he should consult the leader. Unfamiliar descent routes that appear temptingly easy in the upper portions often lead to serious difficulties below. A long climb up again may result.

Caution on Descent

More accidents occur on the descent of long climbs than on the ascent. The reasons include the following: (1) The party often has a false feeling of overconfidence, elation, and relaxation after a successful ascent. (2) The climbers are tired. Both judgment and physical abilities may be impaired. (3) The party is in a hurry to get back to camp. (4) Conditions may be worse. The weather may be threatening, the air cold, and the light poor. Extra care should be practiced.

Techniques of Descent

If the climbing is at all steep, the leader comes down last

to protect his party. In the high mountains the party is more apt to climb down than rappel. Routes are often poorly adapted to rappelling, and rope handling is very time-consuming when climbing and rappelling frequently alternate. On steep, difficult pitches that are particularly uninviting to climb down, a rappel may be preferred. Take special care in selecting the rappel point. Be sure the rope does not send down loose rocks; the first man down should remove any rocks that might easily be dislodged. More frequent belays may be advisable on the descent than on the ascent, and the rope is often kept on longer.

Descending Scree and Talus

On the way up, fine gravel and coarse dirt, known as scree, was probably avoided because of its instability. On the way down, scree should be sought out, as it forms chutes that you can slide, run, or shuffle down. The talus is just about as tedious on the descent as on the ascent, and maybe more so. Certainly, muscles used on the long descent cry out in protest next day. The large talus blocks often seem easier than in the morning, in contrast with the technical climbing.

Travel After Dark

On long climbs (perhaps because you disregarded your calculations to make the peak), you may be benighted. On technical terrain, climbing after dark is so dangerous that you should normally stop till morning. On non-technical ground, you can campward "plod your weary way." Go as fast as you can while you can still see, as progress is very slow after dark. Vision adjusts well in gradually failing light, and there is often enough light with moon, stars, snow, and pale rocks to continue without using the flashlight. On cloudy nights, in the woods, or on rather tricky footing, the time comes when you have to use the flashlight for safety. Once it is turned on, you usually must continue to use it because in the sharp contrast of dark and light, your vision no longer adjusts to dim light. Travel by flashlight on uneven ground brings up a new set of inconveniences to slow down the long trek, especially because there is usually only one light per party. At least during night travel a climber makes the character-building discovery that, although his knees are literally buckling with exhaustion, he can keep right on going for as many hours as need be.

Bivouacs

As used by climbers, the term "bivouac" means to spend a night out on the technical part of the climb. Planned bivouacs are made by expert climbers on long difficult routes which take more than one day; they carry special equipment such as down clothing, extra water, and (on vertical cliffs) hammocks to sleep in. This type of route is beyond the scope of advanced beginners and intermediate climbers. A bivouac as described here means to spend the night out on snow or rock without planning to.

Preparation

In one sense there is no preparation for an unplanned stay.

In another sense, seasoned climbers always have provisions in their packs for just such emergencies: dry socks, mittens, a stocking cap, an extra sweater or wool shirt, extra food. Bivouacking in a storm is a serious matter, and should be assiduously avoided, but a plastic sleeve or sheet can mitigate the ordeal. If caught out, put on *all* your clothing *before* you get chilled; if you wait too long, you may not even be able to get into it.

Choosing a Bivouac Spot

Unless you are racing darkness and it is nip and tuck whether you can get off the difficult climbing by dark, you should pick out a passably comfortable place before the last minute.

On snow, find bare rocks to sit on if you can. If it is windy, get some sort of shelter from the wind; a hole dug in the snow can help and sometimes a shallow crevasse is found. Use your equipment for insulation. You can sit on the rope. Take special care of your feet; the toes are usually the first thing to freeze. Remove your crampons, as they conduct heat away from your feet. Socks worn all day are damp from perspiration if from nothing else; now is the moment for the dry socks you have carried on so many trips. Wiggle your toes very frequently. Feet can be put in the rucksack for insulation, or you and your friends can take turns warming each other's feet under clothing.

On rock, look for a ledge big enough so you can move around, or at least big enough so you can sit or even lie down in reasonable comfort. If the ledge is at all skimpy, anchor yourselves and all your equipment; and periodically during the night check the knots of your waist loops. Huddle together for mutual warmth. Take turns in the middle unless one person particularly needs that extra bit of warmth. It is strange but true that you probably will sleep part of the time. It will be a long, cold night, devoid of physical comfort. It will also be a rather wonderful night, with a view you will never see again under similar circumstances. Even your mutual sufferings will be hilarious in retrospect.

Resuming Descent

In the morning, allow for the fact that you are pretty well petrified from the cold and the cramped position. Do not start right down as soon as you can see. Move around if it is safe; stretch and eat a little. If you are facing east, wait until the sun reaches you; it comes early on the heights. Descend with extreme caution until you are off the exposed part of the route.

As you pack out, you will look back with satisfaction and pleasure at the peak, which already seems far away. You will trace the route with your eyes, and relive the adventure in your mind and muscles. Sooner or later someone you meet will ask how much "they" paid you to make the climb. You will laugh and say you weren't paid anything. But it isn't quite true. Nobody could (or would) buy your hard-earned skills, the risk, and the work involved. But knowing you reached the summit is a private glory beyond price.

chapter eight

Tips on Where to Climb,
At Home and Abroad

A CLIMBER customarily picks out the cliff, aiguille, peak, or boulder of his desire, and attempts to climb it. At times, however, he needs some special information. If there is no one to ask, how can he tell if an unknown route matches his abilities? What restrictions exist in certain areas? What are some of the conditions to expect and prepare for in a foreign country? Solutions to some of these problems are explained in this chapter.

Climbing Classifications

As soon as your climbing career begins, you will hear routes esoterically described by classes, grades, letters, numbers, and decimal points. These are symbols used in various climbing classification systems.

Reasons for Classifying Climbs

Most rating systems indicate briefly the length, difficulty, and equipment needs for a given climb, and provide a basis for comparison between climbs. All systems presuppose that you understand basic climbing techniques and possess general mountaineering competence. The classifications furnish a standard of difficulty for use in climbers' shop talk and guidebooks. They help you choose ascents suitable for your experience, wherever you are climbing. They provide an approximate criterion for judging the development of your technical skill and how it compares with that of others. The grading systems were not devised as a basis of competition among climbers, but sometimes are used as if they had been.

What Classifications Do Not Do

Keep in mind that ratings are based on good conditions, and on individual climbers' abilities and opinions. Also remember that no climb is ever just like another. Use the systems only as a rough guide to difficulty and equipment needs. Do not expect perfect accuracy and uniformity.

How to Understand Rating Systems

First find out what system is used in your local area. Ask climbers and study guidebooks. Familiarize yourself with the symbols used to describe the climbs you have done, and what they mean in terms of climbing difficulty. Compare your own system with the one used in a new area.

Why Several Systems?

Numerous classification systems have existed (and still do)

in various climbing centers. Where a system is firmly established, its proponents understand it perfectly and are
reluctant to adopt a new one. Also, climbs are too diverse
to fit neatly into any one system. Rock climbs lend themselves more readily than glacier climbs to detailed
classification.

Nevertheless, some local systems have greatly changed
because of new techniques, and some have been replaced
with more widely used systems. One reason for a trend
toward uniformity is the growing number of climbers that
travel from one area to another. Although some of the less
well-known systems are still in use, and an occasional new
one crops up, there are now two major climbing classification systems used (either separately or side by side) in most
of the United States and Canada. It seems reasonable that
one or the other will eventually triumph, or that a crossbreed
system will develop. A uniform rating system is also under
consideration by clubs belonging to the UIAA (Union
Internationale des Associations d'Alpinisme), which includes
the American Alpine Club as well as organizations in Japan,
Europe, and elsewhere.

Major Classification Systems

The two leading systems used in the United States and
Canada at present are (1) the Yosemite System (virtually
identical to the American Rating System), and (2) The
National Climbing Classification System (NCCS).

Yosemite (or American Rating) System. This system
began with the old Sierra Club System, which had the
original purpose of indicating equipment needs. The class

number describes the most difficult pitch of the climb. Beginning and intermediate climbers will be primarily concerned with Class 4 and the easier subdivisions of Class 5. As this basic system is still in use, the original classes are listed; later modifications are described thereafter.

Class 1. Hiking. Any footgear adequate.

Class 2. Proper footgear necessary for rough terrain. Occasional handholds used.

Class 3. Scrambling. Hands may be used frequently. Ropes should be available for occasional use.

Class 4. Ropes and belays must be used for safety. Pitons may be required for anchoring belayers.

Class 5. Protection such as pitons or bolts required above the belayer to protect the leader.

Class 6. Pitons or bolts, etc., must be used for direct aid. (Class 6 is not necessarily harder than Class 5.)

As increasingly difficult rock climbing came into vogue with improved equipment, a majority of climbs fell within Class 5 but varied greatly in difficulty. Southern California climbers worked out the Tahquitz Decimal System for subdividing Class 5 and Class 6 climbing categories. Classes 5.0 and 5.1, for instance, refer to easy routes requiring one or more pitons for leader protection; Classes 5.8, 5.9, and 5.10 refer to exceptionally difficult routes, or routes with at least one very difficult pitch. Similar distinctions were applied to Class 6 (direct aid) pitches, from 6.1 to 6.8. The Yosemite System is exactly the same as the Sierra Club and Tahquitz Decimal systems from Class 1 through Class 5.10.

It replaces the Class 6 ratings with the letter "A," standing for Aid, and divides Aid climbs into five categories of increasing difficulty: A1, A2, A3, A4, and A5. Most Aid climbs require a high degree of skill and technical ability.

The Yosemite System adds grades in Roman numerals I through VI, to indicate overall difficulty and provide an approximation of the times involved. Following are the approximate times assigned to the grades:

Grade I.   A few hours (easy).

Grade II. Half a day.

Grade III. Most of a day.

Grade IV. A full day or one-and-a-half days.

Grade V. A day to two days.

Grade VI. Several days.

The grades developed for the specialized conditions in Yosemite are not uniformly applicable elsewhere, and are not used at all where the time element is unimportant (as where all climbs are short). Similarly, Decimal and Aid categories are not always needed.

National Climbing Classification System (NCCS). This system also uses six grades, based on the length and overall difficulty of a climb. The NCCS uses the A1 to A5 classifications too.

The NCCS describes "difficulty" only by giving examples of climbs in major climbing areas that fall within its categories. Conversion to the system is not easy for a climber from an area for which examples are not given. The NCCS makes no recommendations as to equipment, on the basis that such a choice varies according to each climber's concept

of safety requirements. The main difference in its symbols
is the use of a different numerical rating for free (non-Aid)
climbing, with the letter "F" standing for Free (the key to
which system is being quoted). Comparable degrees of
difficulty are:

Yosemite, Sierra Club, and Decimal Ratings	NCCS
Class 1-2	F1
Class 3	F2
Class 4	F3
Class 5.0-5.2	F4
Class 5.3-5.4	F5
Class 5.5-5.6	F6
Class 5.7 through 5.10	F7 through F10

There is little room for a mix-up at the very bottom of the
scale, or in the top half. But the range between Yosemite or
Decimal Class 3 to 5.2 as compared with NCCS F2 to F4
might very well be confusing. Too, it is this very range that
applies to the beginning and intermediate climber, who might
not have the experience to tell by looking at the climb what
he was getting into.

The theoretical ascent described in Chapter Seven could
be Yosemite Grade III, with pitches of Class 3, Class 4, and
Class 5.1 difficulty; or NCCS Grade III, with F2, F3, and F4
pitches. The rating that might appear in a guidebook using
both systems would be "III, 5.1, F4."

Whatever system you use, let your own observation,
experience, and enjoyment be the deciding factors in choosing and making a climb.

Climbing Regulations

There are few restrictions as to where you may climb in the
United States, beyond your own good judgment. However,
in a few areas, including some with especially fine rock or
mountain terrain, you must have special qualifications and
obtain permission to climb.

Private Property

If you want to climb in areas which are on private
property, or are reached by crossing private property, seek
the owner's permission. Explain your activities, as he may
consider them odd.

Indian Reservations

Peaks and pinnacles often have a serious religious signifi-
cance to the Indians, and should not be ascended without
specific permission.

National Parks and Monuments

Several major national parks and some monuments
regulate climbing activities, officially for reasons of safety.
Climbers generally accept the advisability of registering
before and after climbs, but it is a moot point among them
whether certain other restrictions are justified or effective.
However, the regulations do exist, and must be complied
with. For instance, to get permission to climb Mt. Rainier, a
heavily glaciated peak in a national park, unguided parties
must: (1) Submit a list of each person's previous experience

on similar glacier peaks. (2) Be in good physical condition. (3) Demonstrate that they are outfitted with proper clothing and equipment. (4) Give proof of leadership qualifications and overall strength of party. (5) Have written permission from parents or guardians for all persons under twenty-one. (6) Include in the party at least two ropes of two, or one of three.

National parks that regulate climbing, camping, or both, include Rainier (Washington), Yosemite (California), Rocky Mountain (Colorado), McKinley (Alaska), Zion (Utah), Grand Teton (Wyoming), and Devil's Tower National Monument (Wyoming). If you plan to climb in these areas or in other national parks, write well ahead of time for a list of current regulations. Check with rangers on arrival. Always sign out before starting a climb and in again when you return, at park headquarters or other designated place.

Climbing in Foreign Countries

After gaining basic experience in the United States, you may have the opportunity and urge to climb in foreign countries. Mountains are mountains, but climate, conditions, customs, and sources of information naturally vary. A distinct complication in obtaining information is language, though climbers everywhere usually do their best to help one another. There are, of course, countless ranges in the world. Your first foreign climbs are most apt to be in either North America or Europe, and a few pointers may help.

Canada

In western Canada, of course, Americans have no language

problem. Striking ranges, impressive for beauty, variety, and extensive glaciers, run north and south in the provinces of British Columbia and Alberta. Many well-known peaks lie within the boundaries of Banff and Jasper national parks, but these comprise only a sampling of the whole array.

Type of Climbing and Weather. The mountains catch heavy precipitation, although the intervening valleys may be quite dry. In some places, glacier climbing is accessible from the highway or by trail. In other areas, peaks are reached by very long strenuous backpacks, up river valleys and through down timber. Rock varies from the shattered limestone of the Canadian Rockies to the sound granite of peaks protruding from the glaciers of the Bugaboos .in the Purcell Range. Climbers should carry rainproof tents, although a few huts exist and there are shelters in highway campgrounds in the parks. The weather is most apt to be good in July and August, but expect rain and snow at any time.

Sources of Information. Three guidebooks describe climbing in western Canada. They are available through shops and mail order outlets for mountaineers. They are: *A Climber's Guide to the Coastal Ranges of British Columbia* by Dick Culbert, Alpine Club of Canada, Vancouver, B.C., 1963, $4.50; *A Climber's Guide to the Interior Ranges of British Columbia*, edited by W. L. Putnam, American Alpine Club, New York, N.Y., revised edition, 1963, $4.50; and *A Climber's Guide to the Rocky Mountains of Canada* by J. Monroe Thorington, American Alpine Club, New York, N.Y., revised edition, 1966, $6.00.

You can get topographical maps at national park headquarters or by writing to the Map Distribution Office, Department of Mines and Technical Surveys, Ottawa, Ontario.

Information about huts, summer climbing camps, etc., may be obtained through the Alpine Club of Canada, Banff, Alberta. The ACC also publishes the Canadian Alpine Journal annually.

Climbing Regulations. There are few, if any, restrictions on climbing in Canada; but some as to where you may make high camps in the parks. Always check your plans with a park warden (the counterpart of our ranger). Do not fail to sign out for contemplated climbs and sign in upon return; the authorities really worry about your whereabouts, and a car parked for days by the roadside gives scant clue as to what became of you.

Border Regulations. Crossing the border into Canada presents few problems. No passport or any other identification is required. A driver must have a "Canada Non-Resident Inter-Province Motor Vehicle Liability Insurance Card." It is proof of adequate insurance, and should be obtained through your own agent.

Mexico

Climbers are primarily interested in two areas in Mexico: the region of high, glaciated volcanic peaks near Mexico City, and Baja (Lower) California.

Baja California. The landscape is similar to that of southern California, with desert at lower elevations and coniferous forests above. The highest peak in the region is called Picacho del Diablo by climbers, and Cerro de la Encantada on maps. It is 10,125 feet high, and is reached by a long backpack up a spectacular gorge, and an obscure climbing route. Climbing in this area is thoroughly covered in *Camping and Climbing in Baja* by John W. Robinson, La Siesta Press, Glendale, Calif., $2.95.

The Glacier Peaks. The three major peaks (among countless others) are Popocatépetl (Popo), 17,887 feet high; Ixtaccihuatl (Ixta), 17,343 feet high; and Orizaba, 18,700 feet high, the highest point in Mexico. All regular routes are glacier climbs of moderate difficulty. The high elevations add to the exertion. Crampons, ice axes and snow goggles are required; a rope should be carried. The best climbing season is from mid-November through February—the dry season. Climbers from the United States find the Thanksgiving and Christmas holidays admirably synchronized with the Mexican climbing season. Huts serve most of the routes. Take your own stove.

How to Find the Peaks. The peaks are plainly seen, but actually getting to the climbs is complicated by lack of written information, poor road signs, and language problems (Spanish and a variety of Indian dialects are spoken). The following directions will help you get there. Elevations are not well-established, and those given are only approximate.

To get to Popo and Ixta, drive to the town of Amecameca, at an elevation of 7800 feet, about thirty miles southeast of Mexico City. About three-tenths of a mile south of Amecameca, a side road that is sometimes unmarked goes east to the Ixta-Popo National Park and the village of Tlamacas. After entering the park, the road branches at a big monument, at about 12,000 feet.

For Popo, take the righthand branch 6 1/2 miles to a parking area. The Tlamacas (Popo) Hut is about two hours' climb from the car, at 15,500 feet. There is a large main room, and cubicles for 120 climbers. Pure snow water is piped to the hut.

Climbing routes are marked on a chart in the hut. The regular route, Las Cruces, leads up an unbroken snow slope to the lower crater rim, and around the rim to the summit about 500 feet above.

To climb Ixta, take the lefthand branch of the road from the monument. It goes 3 1/2 miles to the roadhead at about 13,300 feet. You can climb the peak from the car, or backpack to any of the three shelters located roughly at 14,000, 15,000, and 16,000 feet. Ixta's huts have no real water supply, but as they are above the usual snowline, water from streams is usually available. The route to the summit is alpine in character, and the best way must be selected among steep snow slopes, rock, and cornices. The summit lies slightly to the right as the climber approaches.

To find Orizaba, drive to the city of Puebla, about 75 miles southeast of Mexico City, and from there another 60 miles or so to San Salvador El Seco.

To climb Orizaba from the north, continue on the main highway for about 5-6 miles, and look for a sandy road to the right that goes to the town of Tlachichuca. At this town, at 8500 feet, a jeep can be rented from the storekeeper (Rios by name) to take you to the hut, a good one with water, at about 14,500 feet. The same man can provide peasant guides. The climb is direct and steep, mostly on glacier. The summit is opposite the first point reached on the crater rim, and about 600 feet higher.

To climb Orizaba from the south, turn southeast at San Salvador El Seco, and drive to the village of Ciudad Serdán (also known as San Andrés Chalchicomula), at 8500 feet. Look up the Jimenez brothers at Callejon Crespo 7. They speak English adequately, will act as guides, and will take your belongings and water in on pack animals. The traditional high camp is at about 14,500 feet, twelve miles from Ciudad Serdán. The campsite is a cave, near timberline, on the west edge of a saddle between Orizaba proper and a prominent cinder cone to the south. From here, the peak can be climbed by any of several steep cinder or snow fields (there are no glaciers on this side). A good route is reached by crossing the saddle partway towards the east. The climb is long, the elevation high, and the days are short during the climbing season; a pre-dawn start is recommended.

Further Climbing Information. Additional information may be obtained by writing to Club de Exploraciones de México, Apartado Postal 10134, México 8, D.F., México.

Health Problems. Tourists to Mexico, as elsewhere, sometimes fall victim to a digestive disorder (known among climbers as Montezuma's Revenge). It is not serious, and of course not everyone gets it; but it could spoil your climbing plans. As a preventive, eat only the food you have along until you are done climbing; and either take your own water, drink bottled water, or use water-purifying tablets (chlorine or iodine types) available at drugstores. As in many places, keep track of your belongings.

Border Regulations. A tourist card, required for more than a brief stay, may be obtained at a Mexican consulate or a Department of Tourism office, or at the border. Proof of United States citizenship is required. Persons under twenty-one must have a letter of permission from parents or guardians. If driving, ask your insurance agent about special requirements; the usual procedure is to buy Mexican coverage at a U.S. border town. Excellent buses go almost everywhere in Mexico.

Europe

Climbing is a popular and respected pursuit in Europe (you won't wonder, when you see the Alps). You will find that several aspects of European mountaineering are quite different from climbing in the United States.

Huts. Backpacking and high camps, an integral part of American climbing, scarcely exist in Europe. There are literally hundreds of well-supplied accommodations, conveniently located for virtually every climb. They exist primarily or solely for the comfort and safety of climbers. Most of these huts belong to the large Alpine clubs, some to government agencies. A long hike or climb is often necessary to reach the huts, but once you are there, you are supplied with shelter, blankets, pillows, and usually any meals you wish. There is no need for a sleeping bag at the huts, and there is no use for a packframe at all. A rucksack easily holds all your needs: climbing equipment, clothing, and personal belongings. The huts and refuges range from small ones for seldom climbed routes or emergency shelters, to large hotels. Accommodations may be dormitories or "mattress rooms," bunk rooms for four to six people, or even private rooms with sheets on the beds. The more modest beds cost somewhere between 50¢ to $1.50 per person per night. Service at the huts includes being waked up and fed at about 3 A.M. on climbing days.

Food and Water at Huts. You can take all or part of your own food, cook it yourself or have it cooked for you, or order all your meals at many of the huts. An economical and satisfactory system is to purchase rucksack foods—bread, butter, cheese, sausage, sugar, tea bags or instant coffee, etc., for breakfasts and lunches—at the towns below, and order soups, beverages, and dinners at the huts. Dinners vary in price from about 50¢ to $1.75, depending on where you are and what you eat. All sorts of beverages (including wines) are available, except the plain cold water that Americans are used to. Order hot water by the liter for tea or coffee; it costs about 12¢ to 30¢, including cups. As real water supplies are often either lacking or questionable, it is usually best to drink only heated or bottled water, or carry water-purifying tablets. Store your extra tea water in a water bottle for future use.

Clothing and Miscellany Needed. Most European climbers appear better dressed than bushwhacking, camping Americans. To be in style, wear long socks and knickers (corduroy knickers are popular, though wool or nylon is more water-repellent). Expect cold, wet weather, even during July and August, the best months. A plastic raincoat or poncho is essential. For some huts you need slippers or extra shoes, as climbing boots are forbidden for indoor wear. You should provide spare pants in case yours get wet, since huts are usually unheated in summer. A small foreign language dictionary is useful, as are reading and writing materials for stormy days.

Gathering Information. Some of the things you need to know are best looked into before leaving home, others at the European climbing centers. For road maps, send to the Esso Touring Service, Foreign Dept., 15 W. 51st St., New York, N.Y. Tourist offices in the United States can provide some information about European climbing centers. Climber's guidebooks in French or German are prolific in Europe, but the few available in English should be obtained here or in England. The Alpine Club of England is publishing a new series of pocket guides, covering "selected climbs" in portions of the Alps. These cost between $3.50 and $7.50 each, and are available in mountaineering shops. Also, find out all you can from friends who have climbed in the Alps.

When you arrive in a European town near your selected climbs, go to the tourist or information bureau, or climbing club office, to make inquiries about local huts. The "approach" to the hut may combine a trip by car, funicular, and cog railway, and walking or climbing. Railways serve many areas not reached by roads. Topographical maps showing roads, railways, funiculars, trails, huts, peaks, and elevations (in meters) can be purchased at tourist bureaus or book stores. If you have no one to climb with, or are inexperienced, guides can be hired at climbing centers and will take care of all arrangements. Of course, European climbers are glad to help you if you can break the language barrier. By no means all Europeans speak English; those who do often reach a point where they can go no further—your own situation exactly, with languages learned in school. At this point, speak English slowly, repeat as necessary, avoid idioms, and try synonyms. At least everyone has a laugh.

On good climbing days, popular routes on well-known peaks are usually easy to find. They are apt to be quite crowded with both guided and amateur parties of several nationalities.

Climbing Equipment. Whether to take your own clothing

and equipment, or to rent it or buy it abroad, poses a problem. It depends on the state of your own equipment, your travel weight allowance, and your finances. You will certainly want to buy at least *some* outing equipment. The mountaineering shops are wonderful. Climbing footgear is sold also in many shoe stores. Clothing purchased and *worn* in Europe is duty-free. And remember that much equipment sold in the United States has been imported, and might preferably be selected in Europe and if necessary shipped home by mail or freight.

Foreign Climbing Clubs. There are far too many climbing and outing clubs abroad to list them all. Membership in a European Alpine club entitles you to greatly reduced rates for food and lodging at the club huts, and is worthwhile for a long stay. Some major Alpine clubs are:

Austria. Österreichischer Alpenverein, Gilmstrasse 6, Innsbruck, Austria.

France. Club Alpin Français, Paris-Chamonix Section, 7 Rue la Boétie, Paris 8e, France. Club offices in Chamonix are open during the climbing season.

Germany. Deutscher Alpenverein, Praterinsel 5, München 22, Germany.

Great Britain. The Alpine Club, 74 S. Audley St., London, W1, England; Fell and Rock Climbing Club of the English Lake District, Cheshire, England (publishes guides to various sections of the Lake District); Association of Scottish Climbing Clubs, 406 Sauchiehall, Glasgow C2, Scotland.

Italy. Club Alpino Italiano, Torino, Italy.

Switzerland. Schweizer Alpenclub, Steinenvorstadt 36, Basel, Switzerland.

Mountaineering clubs, climbing guidebooks, and other sources of information for the United States will be listed in the next chapter.

chapter nine

Sources of Information
For Mountain Climbers

CLUBS for climbers and mountaineers abound in the United States. General outdoor clubs often have special climbing sections, and a few large associations include widely scattered chapters. Most colleges and universities have active outing or climbing clubs; these are not listed here. Many climbing groups present programs, show slides of climbing areas, and publish news sheets, bulletins, annual journals, guidebooks, or other informative material about climbs and mountains. Most offer formal or informal instruction. Representative climbing clubs from diverse parts of the country are listed, but there are many more.

Climbing Clubs

Alaska. Mountaineering Club of Alaska, 700 5th Ave., Anchorage.

Arizona. Kachina Mountain Club, 2217 Encanto Dr., N.W., Phoenix.

California. Sierra Club, 1050 Mills Tower, San Francisco. (Nationwide chapters. San Francisco Bay, Los Angeles, and San Diego chapters have large, active climbing groups.)

Colorado. Colorado Mountain Club, 1723 E. 16th Ave., Denver. (Several sections.)

District of Columbia. Potomac Appalachian Trail Club, Mountaineering Section, 1718 N St., N.W., Washington.

Hawaii. Hawaiian Trail and Mountain Club, P.O. Box 2238, Honolulu.

Idaho. Idaho Alpine Club, P.O. Box 2885, Idaho Falls.

Illinois. Chicago Mountaineering Club, 2901 S. Parkway, Chicago.

Iowa. Iowa Mountaineers, P.O. Box 163, Iowa City.

Maryland. Mountain Club of Maryland, 3220 Brightwood Ave., Baltimore.

Massachusetts. Appalachian Mountain Club, 5 Joy St., Boston. (Many chapters.) New England Trail Conference, Box 241, Princeton. (Affiliated groups.)

Montana. Rocky Mountaineer Club, 2100 South Ave. W., Missoula.

New Mexico. New Mexico Mountain Club, P.O. Box 4151, Albuquerque.

New York. Adirondack Mountain Club, Inc., Gabriels. American Alpine Club, 113 E. 90th St., New York. (Regional sections. Does not sponsor outings.)

Oregon. Mazamas, 909 N.W. 19th Ave., Portland.

Utah. Wasatch Mountain Club, 425 S. 8th W., Salt Lake City.

Washington. The Mountaineers, P.O. Box 122, Seattle. Spokane Mountaineers, Inc., P.O. Box 1013, Spokane.

Guide Services

Several commercial guide services conduct climbing schools in vacation and climbing centers. Write for information on courses, dates, equipment, and fees. A few representative services follow.

Exum Mountain Guide Service and School of American Mountaineering, Moose, Wyo.

Mountaineering Guide Service, P.O. Box 327, Big Pine, Calif.

Mount Rainier Guiding Service, 1525 11th Ave., Seattle, Wash.

Rocky Mountain Guide Service and Mountaineering School, Inc., 1250 S. St. Vrain Highway, Estes Park, Colo.

Sources of Equipment Information

A visit to a local shop carrying mountaineering equipment is instructive and pleasant. If such stores do not rate a mountaineering heading in the telephone book, look under sporting goods, camping equipment, or skiing. Some of the mountaineering firms that publish informative catalogues of specialized equipment are listed.

Alpine Hut, 4725 30th Ave., N.E., Seattle, Wash.

Chouinard, P.O. Box 150, Ventura, Calif.

Gerry, Box 910, Boulder, Colo.

Holubar Mountaineering, Ltd., 1030 13th St., Boulder, Colo.

Matterhorn, Inc., P.O. Box 669, Silver Spring, Md.

Recreational Equipment, Inc., 1525 11th Ave., Seattle, Wash.

The Ski Hut, 1615 University Ave., Berkeley, Calif.

Sport Chalet, Box 626, La Canada, Calif.

Wilderness House, 1310-A Commonwealth Ave., Boston, Mass.

Books, Journals, and Periodicals

A large body of fine mountaineering literature deals with classical climbs, expeditions, adventures, tragedies, ascents, and mountain philosophies the world over. These engrossing books are found in libraries, book stores, and mountaineering shops. They are not listed here; you will discover them for yourself.

Publications of practical and current interest to newcomers in the climbing world include instructional material, regional guidebooks and maps, annual journals of climbing clubs, and the one independent mountaineering magazine in the United States. The list below is not all-inclusive; you will find other useful and absorbing reading material as you browse.

Books of Mountaineering Instruction

Belaying the Leader, an Omnibus on Climbing Safety, Dick Leonard, ed. Sierra Club, San Francisco, Calif. 1956. $1.95.

Mountaineering, The Freedom of the Hills, Climbing Committee of the Mountaineers. The Mountaineers, Seattle, Wash. 2nd ed., 1967. $7.50.

Ropes, Knots and Slings for Climbers, by Walt Wheelock; revised by Royal Robbins. La Siesta Press, Glendale, Calif. Revised ed., 1967. $1.00.

Books for Mountain Emergencies

The ABC of Avalanche Safety, by E. R. Chappelle. Highlander Publishing Co., Boulder, Colo. 1961. 75¢.

Being Your Own Wilderness Doctor, by E. Russel Kodet, M.D., and Bradford Angier. The Stackpole Co., Harrisburg, Pa., 1968. $3.95.

Medicine for Mountaineering, James A. Wilkerson, M.D., ed. The Mountaineers, Seattle, Wash. 1967. $7.50.

Mountain Rescue Techniques, by Wastl Mariner. Österreichischer Alpenverein, Vienna. English translation, The Mountaineers, Seattle, Wash. 2nd ed., 1965. $3.50.

Mountaineering Medicine (First Aid for Outdoorsmen), by Fred T. Darville, Jr., M.D. Skagit Mountain Rescue Unit, Inc., Mount Vernon, Wash. Revised ed., 1966. $1.00.

Books on Approach and Camping

All about Camping, by W. K. Merrill. The Stackpole Co., Harrisburg, Pa. 1963. $4.95.

Backpack Cookery, by Ruth Dyar Mendenhall. La Siesta Press, Glendale, Calif. 1966. $1.00.

Backpack Techniques, by Ruth Dyar Mendenhall. La Siesta Press, Glendale, Calif. 1967. $1.00.

Home in Your Pack, by Bradford Angier. The Stackpole Co., Harrisburg, Pa. 1965. $4.50.

Skills for Taming the Wilds, by Bradford Angier. The Stackpole Co., Harrisburg, Pa. 1967. $6.95.

Representative Club Publications

Accidents in North American Mountaineering. Annual report of the Safety Committee of the American Alpine Club, New York, N.Y. 75¢.

American Alpine Club Journal. Annual. American Alpine Club, New York, N.Y. $5.00.

Appalachia. June and December magazines. Appalachian Mountain Club, Boston, Mass. Subscription to biannual magazine, $3.50 a year.

Ascent, Sierra Club Mountaineering Journal. Annual. Sierra Club, San Francisco, Calif. $2.50.

Periodicals

Summit, A Mountaineering Magazine. Big Bear Lake, Calif. Monthly. Subscriptions, $6.00 a year.

Climbers' Guidebooks

A Climber's Guide to the Adirondacks (Rock Climbing), Trudy Healy, ed. Adirondack Mountain Club, Gabriels, N.Y. 1967. $2.50.

A Climber's Guide to the Cascade and Olympic Mountains of Washington, Cascade Section of the American Alpine Club. American Alpine Club, New York, N.Y. 2nd ed., 1961. $5.00.

A Climber's Guide to Glacier National Park, by J. Gordon Edwards. Sierra Club, San Francisco, Calif. Revised ed., 1966. $4.75.

A Climber's Guide to the High Sierra, Hervey H. Voge, ed. Sierra Club, San Francisco, Calif. Revised ed., 1965. $4.75.

A Climber's Guide to Oregon, by Nicholas A. Dodge. Mazamas, Portland, Ore. 1968. $3.95.

A Climber's Guide to Pinnacles National Monument, by Steve Roper. The Ski Hut, Berkeley, Calif. 1966. $2.75.

A Climber's Guide to the Quincy Quarries, by William R. Crowther and Anthony W. Thompson. M.I.T. Outing Club, Cambridge, Mass. 1968. 60¢.

A Climber's Guide to the Shawangunks, by Arthur Gran. American Alpine Club with The Appalachian Mountain Club (New York chapter), New York, N.Y. 1964. $5.00.

A Climber's Guide to Tahquitz Rock, by Chuck Wilts. La Siesta Press, Glendale, Calif. 3rd ed., 1962. $2.75.

A Climber's Guide to the Teton Range, by Leigh Ortenburger. Sierra Club, San Francisco, Calif. Revised ed., 1965. $6.00.

A Climber's Guide to Yosemite Valley, by Steve Roper. Sierra Club, San Francisco, Calif. 1964. $4.75.

Guide to Adirondack Trails. Adirondack Mountain Club, Gabriels, N.Y. 7th ed., 1962. $3.25.

Guide to the Colorado Mountains, by Robert Ormes. Colorado Mountain Club, Denver, Colo. 4th ed., 1963. $3.50.

Guide to Leavenworth Rock Climbing Areas, by Fred Beckey and Eric Bjornstad. The Mountaineers, Seattle, Wash. 1965. $2.50.

Guide to the Mississippi Palisades, by James Kolocotronis. Iowa Mountaineers, Iowa City, Iowa. 1965. $1.00.

Guide to the New Mexico Mountains, by Herbert E. Ungnade. Sage Books, Denver, Colo. 1965. $3.95.

Guide to the Wyoming Mountains and Wilderness Areas, by Orrin H. Bonney and Lorraine Bonney. Sage Books, Denver, Colo. 2nd revised ed., 1965. $7.50.

Maine Mountain Guide Book. Appalachian Mountain Club, Boston, Mass. 2nd ed., 1968. $4.50.

White Mountain Guide. Appalachian Mountain Club, Boston, Mass. 19th ed., 1969. $5.00.

Maps

Pertinent maps for an area are usually included in guidebooks. Most such maps should be augmented by topographical maps of the United States Geodetic Survey. These can be purchased in map or mountaineering stores, or by mail from the U.S. Geodetic Survey, Denver, Colo. 80225 or Washington, D.C. 20242. Various Forest Service and national park headquarters can often provide large-scale topo maps useful for the specific area.

Index

(*Note:* Page numbers in italics refer to illustrations.)